GRANDMA'S TOUCH
Tasty, Traditional & Tempting

by Irene Hrechuk
& Verna Zasada

Front Cover: Crumb-Topped Pie, page 129

GRANDMA'S TOUCH
by
Irene Hrechuk & Verna Zasada

First Printing — January 1990
Second Printing — August 1990
Third Printing — April 1991
Fourth Printing — October 1991
Fifth Printing — November 1992
Sixth Printing — October 1993
Seventh Printing — September 1994
Eighth Printing — June 1996
Ninth Printing — June 1999
Tenth Printing — June 2000

Canadian Cataloguing in Publication Data

Hrechuk, Irene, 1943 —
    Grandma's Touch

    ISBN 0-919845-79-7
1. Cookery. I. Zasada, Verna, 1934 —
II Title.

TX725.A1H73   1990   641.5   C90-097016-2

Photography by
Merle Prosofsky
Merle Prosofsky Photography
Edmonton, Alberta

Dishes and Accessories Compliments of:
Birks Jewellers

Designed, Printed and Produced in Canada by:
Centax Books, a Division of PrintWest Communications Ltd.
Publishing Director, Photo Designer & Food Stylist: Margo Embury
1150 Eighth Avenue, Regina, Saskatchewan, Canada   S4R 1C9
(306) 525-2304   Fax: (306) 757-2439
E-mail: centax@printwest.com   www.centaxbooks.com

TABLE OF CONTENTS

INTRODUCTION

"Grandma's Touch" authors, Irene Hrechuk and Verna Zasada, grew up with the wonderful flavors and aromas of Norwegian, English, Ukrainian, Polish and "Canadian" food. Their rich cultural and culinary heritage has been enhanced by exchanging treasured family recipes with friends from many cultural groups. "Grandma's Touch" represents the multicultural aspect of Canadian life and includes family favorites from British, Chinese, French, German, Italian, Irish, Mexican, Norwegian, Polish, Russian, Scandinavian and Ukrainian grandmothers.

These family-style recipes will be appreciated by beginning cooks, for their simplicity and they will be prized by experienced cooks, for their quality. The recipes in "Grandma's Touch" have been updated for today's busy, health-conscious cooks. They use few packaged ingredients so each cook can control the amount of salt, fat, sugar and cholesterol, according to her family's needs. These recipes are economical, easy-to-prepare, nutritious, use readily available ingredients and, best of all, they are delicious!

Variations and substitutions are included with many basic recipes. These suggestions make the recipes more versatile and they inspire the novice cooks to branch out and adapt recipes on their own.

As we begin to move into the twenty-first century, and the world becomes a global village, we can draw on more and more sophisticated recipes and exotic ingredients from around the world. Today's hectic lifestyle pushes us towards fast-food outlets at an increasing rate. "Grandma's Touch" gives us a change of pace and a taste of nostalgia in these well-loved foods from our childhood. Remember your special childhood favorites as grandma and great grandma used to make them? Here are the satisfying, comforting flavors and aromas that you remember from grandma's kitchen.

Brunch & Breads

Indulge your family and guests with these
simple, nutritious brunch dishes.
Make any meal a special occasion with
hot-from-the-oven, homemade biscuits,
muffins, loaves and buns.
Give a gift of love and warmth
with your favorite breads and muffins.

OVEN-BAKED OMELET

HERE IS A COLORFUL BREAKFAST DISH WITH LOTS OF FLAVOR

2 tbsp.	butter	30 mL
2 cups	hash brown potatoes	500 mL
¼ tsp.	salt	1 mL
¼ tsp.	pepper	1 mL
1 tbsp.	butter	15 mL
½ cup	chopped onion	125 mL
½ cup	chopped green pepper	125 mL
½ cup	chopped mushrooms	125 mL
2 tsp.	flour	10 mL
¾ cup	chopped ham OR other cooked meat	175 mL
3	eggs	3
½ cup	milk	125 mL
½ cup	grated cheese	125 mL

- In skillet, melt 2 tbsp. (30 mL) butter. Add potatoes. Cook, stirring frequently, until brown. Add salt and pepper. Line the bottom and sides of a greased 10" (25 cm) pie plate with the potatoes.
- In skillet, melt 1 tbsp. (15 mL) butter; cook onion, pepper and mushrooms until tender. Stir in flour and meat.
- Beat eggs and milk together. Add to meat-vegetable mixture. Pour into potato-lined plate.
- Bake at 350°F (180°C) for 20 minutes. Remove and sprinkle cheese on top. Bake an additional 10 minutes or until omelet is set and cheese melted.

YIELD   *4 SERVINGS*

BREAKFAST BAKE

A TREAT FOR ANY BRUNCH BECAUSE IT IS PREPARED THE NIGHT BEFORE
GREAT FOR CHRISTMAS MORNING!

10	slices bread, cubed	10
6	eggs, lightly beaten	6
3 cups	milk	750 mL
¾ tsp.	dry mustard	3 mL
2 cups	grated Cheddar OR Swiss cheese	500 mL
1 tbsp.	parsley	15 mL
2 cups	cubed ham	500 mL

- Place cubed bread in the bottom of a buttered 8 x 12" (20 x 30 cm) pan.
- Combine the remaining ingredients and pour mixture over the bread.
- Cover and refrigerate overnight.
- Bake, uncovered, at 350°F (180°C) for 1 hour.
- Remove from oven and let sit 5 minutes before cutting.

VARIATIONS *Bacon or sausages may be used in place of ham.*
Sliced tomatoes and mushrooms may be added if desired.

YIELD **8-10 SERVINGS**

BAKED CANADIAN BACON

2 lbs.	back bacon	1 kg
½ cup	brown sugar	125 mL
½ tsp.	dry mustard	2 mL
½ cup	unsweetened pineapple juice	125 mL

- Place bacon in a shallow roasting pan.
- Combine sugar, mustard and pineapple juice. Spread mixture over bacon.
- Bake, uncovered, at 325°F (160°C) for 1 hour, basting with pan juices every 15 minutes.

YIELD   *8 SERVINGS*

ORANGE FRENCH TOAST

1	loaf French bread, cut into 1" (2.5 cm) slices	1
4	eggs	4
¾ cup	heavy cream	175 mL
¼ cup	orange juice	50 mL
1 tsp.	grated orange rind	5 mL
½ tsp.	vanilla	2 mL
⅛ tsp.	nutmeg	0.5 mL
	icing (confectioner's) sugar	
	syrup OR jam	

- Arrange bread slices in a shallow pan.
- Combine eggs, cream, orange juice and rind, vanilla and nutmeg, blending well. Pour over bread slices. Turn slices over to absorb mixture.
- Place slices on a greased cookie sheet. Bake in a preheated 500°F (260°C) oven for 5 minutes on each side or until golden brown.
- While warm sprinkle toast with icing sugar.
- Serve toast with syrup, Blueberry-Rhubarb Sauce, page 39, jam or whipped cream, accompany with fresh fruit, blueberries, strawberries, etc..

YIELD   *4-6 SERVINGS*

See photograph opposite page 16.

BASIC PANCAKE BATTER

FROM THIS BASIC RECIPE YOU CAN MAKE AN INFINITE VARIETY OF PANCAKES

2 cups	flour	500 mL
2 tsp.	baking powder	10 mL
1 tsp.	baking soda	5 mL
½ tsp.	salt	2 mL
2 cups	milk OR sour milk* OR buttermilk	500 mL
⅓ cup	cooking oil	75 mL
2	eggs	2

- Combine dry ingredients in a mixing bowl.
- Make a well in dry ingredients and add milk, oil and eggs. Stir until just blended.
- Drop batter in ¼ cup (50 mL) portions onto a hot skillet. When bubbles begin to appear on top, flip to brown the other side.
- Serve with butter, syrup and/or brown sugar and cinnamon.

* To make sour milk, place 2 tbsp. (30 mL) lemon juice or vinegar in a measuring cup, fill cup with milk.

VARIATIONS
— *Substitute ⅔ cup (150 mL) oat bran for ⅔ cup (150 mL) of flour.*
— *Try adding 1 cup (250 mL) of corn niblets or blueberries or banana, peach or apple slices to pancake batter, just before cooking pancakes.*
— *Try Bacon Cheese Pancakes, add 6 slices of crisp, crumbled bacon and 1 cup (250 mL) grated Cheddar cheese to pancake flour.*
— *Serve pancakes, rolled up or layered, with your favorite fruit or fruit preserves. For a touch of luxury add a dollop of whipped cream.*

YIELD   *16, 5" (13 cm) ROUND PANCAKES*

CRÊPES

USE AS A BRUNCH DISH, A PARTY APPETIZER,
A MAIN COURSE, OR A MEMORABLE DESSERT!

4	eggs	4
1 cup	flour	250 mL
½ tsp.	salt	2 mL
1 cup	milk	250 mL
½ cup	water	125 mL
1 tsp.	oil	5 mL

- Beat eggs until light and fluffy. Add remaining ingredients. Beat until smooth. Let batter rest for 2 hours or overnight.
- Heat a lightly greased 6" (15 cm) frying pan. Spoon in about 2 tbsp. (30 mL) of batter or enough to lightly cover the bottom of the pan. Return pan to heat and brown lightly, until crêpe is firm to touch on the top. Remove to a platter, placing a piece of waxed paper between each crêpe, and keep warm until all batter is used.
- Fill crêpes with 1 of the following fillings or freeze for future use.

YIELD   **APPROX. 24 CRÊPES**

COTTAGE CHEESE FILLING

24	crêpes	24
2 cups	cottage cheese	500 mL
2	egg yolks	2
2 tbsp.	whipping cream	30 mL
¼ tsp.	salt	1 mL
¼ tsp.	pepper	1 mL
1 tsp.	dillweed	5 mL
2	green onions, chopped	2
	butter OR whipping cream	

- Prepare crêpes as above.
- Combine all ingredients, except butter. Place 1 tbsp. (15 mL) of filling on each crêpe. Roll up crêpes and place in a buttered 9 x 13" (23 x 32 cm) baking dish. Dot crêpes with butter or whipping cream. Bake in a 350°F (180°C) oven for 30 minutes or until thoroughly heated.

VARIATIONS   *For cottage cheese dessert crêpes, omit the salt, pepper, dillweed and onion. Add 1 tbsp. (15 mL) of sugar. Serve topped with a warm sauce such as Blueberry-Rhubarb Sauce, page 39.*

Spinach Mushroom Crêpe Filling

24	crêpes	24
¼ cup	butter	50 mL
⅓ cup	flour	75 mL
3 cups	hot milk	750 mL
½ tsp.	salt	2 mL
¼ tsp.	nutmeg	1 mL
¼ tsp.	pepper	1 mL
¼ cup	whipping cream	50 mL
1 cup	grated Swiss cheese	250 mL
1½ cups	sliced mushrooms	375 mL
2 tbsp.	butter	30 mL
1½ cups	cooked chopped spinach	375 mL

- Prepare crêpes as on page 10.
- In a saucepan, melt ¼ cup (50 mL) butter. Add flour and blend well. Remove from heat. Using a whisk, add hot milk and seasonings, blending well . Return sauce to low heat. Stir in cream and all but 2 tbsp. (30 mL) of cheese. Simmer for 3 minutes while stirring. Then set aside.
- Sauté mushrooms in remaining 2 tbsp. (30 mL) butter. Remove from heat. Add spinach and ¼ cup (50 mL) of sauce to mushrooms. Mix well.
- Place 1 tbsp. (15 mL) of spinach-mushroom filling on each crêpe. Roll up crêpes and place in a buttered 9 x 13" (23 x 32 cm) baking dish. Pour remaining sauce over crêpes. Sprinkle remaining cheese on top. Bake at 350°F (180°C) for 30 minutes or until thoroughly heated.

Banana-Chocolate Crêpes

8	crêpes	8
4	bananas	4
1 cup	chocolate sauce	250 mL

- Prepare crêpes as on page 10.
- Peel bananas and slice lengthwise. Roll each banana half in a crêpe. Top each crêpe with 2 tbsp. (30 mL) chocolate sauce.

YIELD   *8 SERVINGS*

HINTS   *"Resting" time for crêpe batter allows the flour to absorb more liquids, makes the batter easier to handle and adds flavor.*

YORKSHIRE PUDDING

THIS RECIPE CAME FROM AN IRISH FRIEND WHO SHARES HER HINTS
FOR PERFECT YORKSHIRE PUDDING!

2	eggs	2
1 cup	milk	250 mL
1 cup	flour	250 mL
½ tsp.	salt	2 mL
1 tbsp.	warm water	15 mL
	bacon fat *	

- Early in the day, beat eggs, milk, flour and salt together for 3 minutes. Refrigerate.
- In the middle of the day, remove batter from the refrigerator and beat again; refrigerate batter.
- Just prior to baking, add 1 tbsp. (15 mL) warm water to batter and beat again.
- Put ½ tsp. (2 mL) of bacon fat in each cup of a muffin tin. Place in a 400°F (200°C) oven until fat is hot. While resting muffin tin on opened oven door (to keep fat hot), pour pudding into muffin cups.
- Bake at 400°F (200°C) for 20 minutes or until puffed and browned. Serve immediately.

* When preparing bacon for breakfast save the bacon drippings and refrigerate until needed.

VARIATIONS   *To make Popovers for breakfast or brunch, prepare Yorkshire Pudding batter, grease muffin cups with butter or margarine and dust them with flour, sugar or Parmesan cheese. Serve with fruit preserves, marmalade or cheese.*

YIELD   *6-8 INDIVIDUAL PUDDINGS*

BAKING POWDER BISCUITS

LIGHT AND FLUFFY, THESE BISCUITS ARE PERFECT WITH SOUPS AND SALADS

2 cups	flour	500 mL
4 tsp.	baking powder	20 mL
1 tbsp.	sugar	15 mL
½ tsp.	salt	2 mL
½ cup	shortening	125 mL
¾ cup	milk	175 mL
1	egg, beaten	1

- In a mixing bowl, combine flour, baking powder, sugar and salt.
- With a pastry blender, cut shortening into dry ingredients until the mixture is the consistency of coarse meal.
- Combine the milk and egg. Add gradually to blended mixture to form a soft dough. Knead until well mixed. Chill for 1-3 hours.
- Turn dough out onto a floured surface. Roll out to ¾" (2 cm) thick. Cut out circles with a floured cutter. Place on a greased cookie sheet.
- Bake at 450°F (230°C) for 10-12 minutes.

VARIATIONS
— *For Herb Biscuits, add 2 tbsp. mixed herbs, parsley, basil, oregano, etc. to biscuit dough.*
— *For Cheese Biscuits, add ½-1 cup (125-250 mL) grated sharp Cheddar cheese and a sprinkle of cayenne pepper, omit sugar.*

YIELD   *12 BISCUITS*

HINTS   *If biscuit dough is kneaded inside a large plastic bag it won't stick to hands and it won't dry out when left to chill.*

JOHNNY CAKE

ORIGINALLY CALLED "JOURNEY CAKE", THIS CORNMEAL BREAD IS DELICIOUS
SERVE WARM WITH SYRUP OR COLD WITH HONEY

1 cup	cornmeal	250 mL
½ cup	milk	125 mL
½ cup	shortening	125 mL
½ cup	sugar	125 mL
1⅓ cups	flour	325 mL
2½ tsp.	baking powder	12 mL
1 tsp.	salt	5 mL
1	egg	1
1 cup	milk	250 mL

- Combine cornmeal and milk. Set aside.
- In another bowl, cream shortening and blend in sugar.
- Combine flour, baking powder and salt.
- Mix together the egg and milk.
- Add the dry ingredients, alternately with the liquids, to the creamed mixture.
- Blend in the cornmeal mixture.
- Bake in a greased 9" (23 cm) square pan at 350°F (180°C) for 40-45 minutes.
- Serve cake warm with butter, maple syrup, pancake or fruit syrups or honey.

YIELD   *9 SERVINGS*

Pepper Corn Bread
WHAT A GREAT COMBINATION WITH CHILI OR STEW!

1 cup	melted butter	250 mL
¾ cup	buttermilk	175 mL
1½ cups	creamed corn	375 mL
1 cup	cornmeal	250 mL
1	large onion, chopped	1
2	eggs, beaten	2
½ tsp.	baking soda	2 mL
1½ cups	grated sharp Cheddar cheese	375 mL
3	hot peppers, chopped	3

- In a mixing bowl, combine the butter, buttermilk, corn, cormeal, onion, egg, and baking soda until well blended.
- Pour half the mixture into a greased 9" (23 cm) square pan.
- Sprinkle with half the cheese, all the peppers, then the remaining cheese.
- Pour the remaining batter on top.
- Bake at 350°F (180°C) for 50 minutes.
- Serve warm or cold.

VARIATIONS *Fresh or canned jalapeño peppers may be used alone or in combination with other hot peppers.*

YIELD *10 SERVINGS*

See photograph opposite page 80.

HINTS *When preparing hot peppers wear rubber gloves as the juices irritate the skin and eyes. Don't rub your eyes!*

CHEESE BREAD

TRY THIS CHEESE AND HERB BREAD WITH YOUR FAVORITE SOUP

1	egg, well beaten	1
1 cup	milk	250 mL
1 tbsp.	melted butter	15 mL
2 cups	flour	500 mL
4 tsp.	baking powder	20 mL
1 tbsp.	sugar	15 mL
½ tsp.	onion salt	2 mL
¼ tsp.	garlic powder	1 mL
½ tsp.	oregano	2 mL
¼ tsp.	dry mustard	1 mL
1¼ cups	grated sharp Cheddar cheese	300 mL
1 tbsp.	chopped dill OR parsley (optional)	15 mL

- Combine egg, milk and butter.
- In a mixing bowl, combine the remaining ingredients. Make a well in dry ingredients and add milk mixture. Stir until well blended.
- Spread into a greased 5 x 9" (2 L) loaf pan.
- Bake at 350°F (180°C) for 45 minutes.

YIELD   *12-15 SLICES*

See photograph opposite page 48.

Orange French Toast, page 8
Blueberry Rhubarb Sauce, page 39

BRAN MUFFINS

A ONE-BOWL PREPARATION THAT GIVES YOU FRESH MUFFINS FOR THE NEXT MONTH!

1 cup	butter OR margarine	250 mL
1½ cups	sugar	375 mL
3	eggs	3
3 cups	buttermilk	750 mL
3 cups	bran	750 mL
4 cups	flour	1 L
2½ tsp.	baking powder	12 mL
2 tbsp.	baking soda	30 mL
¼ cup	boiling water	50 mL
1½ tbsp.	molasses (optional)	22 mL
1½ cups	raisins	375 mL

- In a large mixing bowl, combine butter, sugar, eggs, buttermilk, bran, flour, and baking powder. Mix well.
- Dissolve baking soda in boiling water. Add to bran mixture.
- Stir in molasses and raisins until just blended.
- Fill greased muffin tins ⅔ full. Bake at 375°F (190°C) for 25 minutes.
- Batter will keep refrigerated in a covered container for up to 4 weeks.

YIELD   *4 DOZEN MEDIUM MUFFINS THAT FREEZE WELL*

BLUEBERRY ORANGE MUFFINS

SWEET AND TANGY — A GREAT COMBINATION!

½ cup	butter OR margarine	125 mL
¾ cup	sugar	175 mL
2	eggs	2
1 cup	orange yogurt	250 mL
2½ cups	flour	625 mL
2 tsp.	baking powder	10 mL
1 tsp.	baking soda	5 mL
⅛ tsp.	salt	0.5 mL
2 tsp.	grated orange rind	10 mL
1¼ cups	blueberries	300 mL

- Beat together butter, sugar, eggs and yogurt until well blended.
- Combine flour, baking powder, baking soda, salt and rind. Add to the creamed mixture. Fold in blueberries.
- Fill greased muffin tins ⅔ full. Bake at 375°F (190°C) for 20 minutes or until golden brown.

YIELD   *18 MUFFINS*

ORANGE MUFFINS

A FRESH-TASTING MOIST MUFFIN

2	oranges, chopped	2
1 cup	orange juice	250 mL
½ cup	oil	125 mL
2	eggs	2
3 cups	flour	750 mL
2 tsp.	baking powder	10 mL
2 tsp.	baking soda	10 mL
½ tsp.	salt	2 mL
1 cup	sugar	250 mL
½ cup	raisins	125 mL
½ cup	chopped nuts	125 mL

- In a blender or food processor combine oranges, juice, oil and eggs until well blended.
- In a separate bowl, combine flour, baking powder, baking soda, salt and sugar.
- Add the orange mixture to the dry ingredients. Mix well then fold in the raisins and nuts.
- Fill greased muffin tins ⅔ full. Bake at 375°F (190°C) for 20 minutes.

VARIATIONS   *½ cup (125 mL) wheat bran or oat bran may be substituted for ½ cup (125 mL) flour.*

YIELD   *24 MUFFINS*

RHUBARB MUFFINS

THE TARTNESS OF RHUBARB WITH A CRUNCHY SPICY TOPPING

3 cups	diced rhubarb	750 mL
1⅓ cups	whole-wheat flour	325 mL
1⅓ cups	all-purpose flour	325 mL
1 cup	brown sugar	250 mL
1 tsp.	baking soda	5 mL
¼ tsp.	salt	1 mL
1 cup	yogurt OR sour cream	250 mL
½ cup	vegetable oil	125 mL
2	eggs	2
1 cup	chopped nuts	250 mL

TOPPING:

½ cup	brown sugar	125 mL
½ cup	chopped nuts	125 mL
2 tbsp.	butter	30 mL
1 tsp.	cinnamon	5 mL

- In a large mixing bowl, combine rhubarb, flours, brown sugar, baking soda and salt.
- In a separate bowl, blend together yogurt, oil and eggs. Stir into rhubarb mixture just until moistened. Fold in nuts.
- Spoon batter into 24 greased muffin cups.
- Combine topping ingredients. Sprinkle a bit of topping mixture on the top of each muffin.
- Bake at 350°F (180°C) for 25-30 minutes.

YIELD   *24 MUFFINS*

SOUR CREAM COFFEE CAKE

THIS IS AN IDEAL "BAKE 'N' TAKE" CAKE FOR PICNICS OR TO TAKE TO A SICK FRIEND
OR TO SEND TO SCHOOL OR TAKE TO THE OFFICE.

TOPPING:

¼ cup	brown sugar	50 mL
¼ cup	finely chopped nuts	50 mL
1 tsp.	cinnamon	5 mL

BATTER:

½ cup	butter	125 mL
1 cup	sugar	250 mL
2	eggs	2
1½ tsp.	baking powder	7 mL
½ tsp.	baking soda	2 mL
1½ cups	flour	375 mL
1 cup	sour cream	250 mL

- Mix together topping ingredients and then set aside.
- In another mixing bowl, beat together butter and sugar. Add eggs and continue to beat until light and creamy.
- Add baking powder, baking soda, flour and sour cream and beat until well blended.
- Turn ⅔ of batter into well-buttered 9" (23 cm) square pan. Sprinkle with ⅔ of the topping mixture. Carefully swirl knife tip through batter and topping. Add remaining batter. Sprinkle remaining topping over batter.
- Bake at 350°F (180°C) for 30-35 minutes.

YIELD **12-16 SERVINGS**

OVERNIGHT COFFEE CAKE

PREPARE AND REFRIGERATE OVERNIGHT — BAKE FRESH FOR BREAKFAST!

⅔ cup	butter OR margarine	150 mL
1 cup	sugar	250 mL
½ cup	brown sugar	125 mL
2	eggs	2
2 cups	flour	500 mL
1 tsp.	baking powder	5 mL
1 tsp.	baking soda	5 mL
1 tsp.	cinnamon	5 mL
½ tsp.	salt	2 mL
1 cup	buttermilk	250 mL
½ cup	brown sugar	125 mL
½ cup	chopped walnuts	125 mL
½ tsp.	cinnamon	2 mL
½ tsp.	nutmeg	2 mL

- Cream butter. Add sugar and ½ cup (125 mL) brown sugar. Cream until light and fluffy. Add eggs, 1 at a time. Beat well after each addition.
- Combine flour, baking powder, baking soda, cinnamon and salt.
- Add dry ingredients alternately with buttermilk and beat well. Pour batter into a greased and floured 9 x 13" (23 x 32 cm) pan.
- Combine the remaining brown sugar with walnuts, cinnamon and nutmeg. Sprinkle over batter in pan. Refrigerate overnight.
- In the morning, bake at 350°F (180°C) for 45 minutes or until cake springs back when touched lightly in the center.
- Serve warm or cool. An excellent accompaniment is seasonal fruit.

YIELD   **15 SERVINGS**

HINTS   *Substitute 1 cup (250 mL) buttermilk with instant sour milk by placing 1 tbsp. (15 mL) lemon juice or vinegar in a cup and filling cup with fresh milk.*

BANANA GUMDROP LOAF
DESTINED TO BE A GREAT HIT

1¾ cups	flour	425 mL
½ tsp.	baking soda	2 mL
1½ tsp.	baking powder	7 mL
⅛ tsp.	salt	0.5 mL
1 cup	chopped gumdrops	250 mL
¼ cup	oil	50 mL
¾ cup	sugar	175 mL
1	egg	1
1 cup	mashed bananas	250 mL
1 cup	milk	250 mL

- Combine flour, baking soda, baking powder and salt. Add gumdrops.
- In a mixing bowl, beat together oil, sugar and egg. Add bananas and milk. Combine well.
- Add dry ingredients to the banana mixture. Mix well.
- Pour batter into a greased and floured 5 x 9" (13 x 23 cm) loaf pan.
- Bake at 350°F (180°C) for 50 minutes or until an inserted toothpick comes out clean.

VARIATIONS   *Add 1 cup (250 mL) of mixed fruit or add ½ cup (125 mL) of nuts or raisins.*

YIELD   **15 SERVINGS**

HINTS   *Mash overripe bananas, add 1 tsp. (15 mL) of lemon juice and freeze in portions usable for banana cakes and breads. 3 bananas mashed, yields approximately 1 cup (250 mL).*

LEMON LOAF

MORE THAN SPECIAL FOR AFTERNOON TEA

½ cup	butter	125 mL
1 cup	white sugar	250 mL
2	eggs	2
1½ cups	flour	375 mL
1 tsp.	baking powder	5 mL
⅛ tsp.	salt	0.5 mL
2 tbsp.	grated lemon rind	30 mL
½ cup	milk	125 mL
2 tbsp.	white sugar	30 mL
2 tbsp.	lemon juice	30 mL

- Cream butter. Gradually blend in sugar and eggs. Beat until light and fluffy.
- In a separate bowl, blend together flour, baking powder, salt and lemon rind.
- Add dry ingredients to creamed mixture alternately with milk.
- Turn batter into a greased 5 X 9" (13 x 23 cm) loaf pan.
- Bake at 350°F (180°C) for 55-60 minutes or until cake springs back when lightly touched. Cool on cake rack for 5 minutes.
- Combine the sugar and lemon juice. Pierce loaf all over with a skewer and pour lemon mixture over the loaf.
- When cool, remove loaf from pan.

YIELD   **12-15 SERVINGS**

DATE LOAF

GRANDMOTHER'S TIME-SAVING RECIPE MAKES 3 LOAVES THAT FREEZE WELL.

1 lb.	dates, chopped	500 g
3 tbsp.	butter OR margarine	45 mL
3 cups	boiling water	750 mL
1 tbsp.	lemon juice	15 mL
1 tbsp.	grated lemon rind	15 mL
3	eggs	3
2 cups	brown sugar	500 mL
5 cups	flour	1.25 L
¼ tsp.	salt	1 mL
2 tsp.	baking soda	10 mL
1 cup	chopped pecans OR walnuts	250 mL
1 cup	raisins	250 mL
1 tsp.	vanilla	5 mL

DATE LOAF
(CONTINUED)

- In a saucepan, combine dates, butter, water, lemon juice and lemon rind. Boil gently, until dates are soft, and then set to cool.
- In a large mixing bowl, beat eggs and sugar. Add date mixture and blend well.
- Combine flour, salt and baking soda. Add to the liquid mixture.
- Add nuts, raisins and vanilla and mix well.
- Pour batter into 3 well-greased 5 x 9" (13 x 23 cm) loaf pans.
- Bake at 350°F (180°C) for 1 hour or until a toothpick inserted in the center comes out clean.

YIELD   *12-15 SLICES PER LOAF*

APPLESAUCE LOAF
SERVE THIS IN PLACE OF MUFFINS

½ cup	butter OR margarine	125 mL
¾ cup	sugar	175 mL
2	eggs	2
1 tsp.	vanilla	5 mL
2 cups	flour	500 mL
1 tsp.	baking powder	5 mL
1 tsp.	baking soda	5 mL
½ tsp.	salt	2 mL
1 tsp.	cinnamon	5 mL
½ tsp.	nutmeg	2 mL
1 cup	unsweetened applesauce	250 mL
½ cup	chopped walnuts	125 mL

- Cream butter and gradually add sugar. Beat until light and fluffy.
- Add eggs and vanilla. Beat well.
- Combine flour, baking powder, baking soda, salt, cinnamon and nutmeg. Add to the creamed mixture. Blend thoroughly.
- Add applesauce and walnuts. Mix only until well blended.
- Pour batter into a greased and floured 5 x 9" (13 x 23 cm) loaf pan. Let stand 20 minutes before baking.
- Bake at 350°F (180°C) for 1 hour. Cool.
- If sweetened applesauce is used, reduce sugar to ½ cup (125 mL). If desired frost with Easy Fudge Icing, page 149.

YIELD   *15 SERVINGS*

OVERNIGHT BUNS

HERE IS A SOLUTION FOR THE BUSY WOMAN
WHO LIKES TO SERVE HER FAMILY HOME-BAKED BUNS

1 tbsp.	yeast (not fast-rising)	15 mL
1 tsp.	sugar	5 mL
½ cup	warm water	125 mL
1 cup	oil	250 mL
1 tbsp.	salt	15 mL
½ cup	sugar	125 mL
2	eggs	2
3 cups	warm water	750 mL
11 cups	flour	2.6 L
1	egg	1
¼ cup	milk	50 mL

- Soak yeast and 1 tsp. (5 mL) sugar in water for 10 minutes or until risen.
- Beat together oil, salt, sugar and eggs.
- Add the yeast mixture and the warm water. Beat well.
- Add half of the flour and beat well. Knead in the remaining flour.
- Place dough in a large greased bowl, cover with a tea towel, let rise for about 2 hours or until double in size.
- Punch down dough, cover, let rise again.
- Shape dough into buns the size of golf balls. Place on greased cookie sheets. Cover and let rise overnight.
- In the morning, brush the buns with a mixture of 1 egg and ¼ cup (50 mL) milk.
- Bake at 375°F (190°C) for 20 minutes or until golden brown.

YIELD   *8 DOZENS BUNS THAT FREEZE VERY WELL*

Salads
& Sauces

Enjoy these old-fashioned salad favorites.
Use them as a colorful, healthy addition to
your family dinners, picnics and buffets.
Many are time-saving, make-ahead and
carry-along salads, perfect for busy cooks.
Sweet and savory sauces enhance breakfast
and main course dishes.

POTATO SALAD

A GREAT CARRY ALONG FOR AN OUTDOOR PICNIC!

8	potatoes, cooked and diced	8
4	hard-boiled eggs, peeled and diced	4
½ cup	chopped celery	125 mL
½ cup	chopped green pepper	125 mL
¼ cup	chopped green onion	50 mL
½ cup	chopped radish	125 mL
⅓ cup	mayonnaise	75 mL
1 tbsp.	prepared mustard	15 mL
2 tbsp.	vinegar	30 mL
1 tsp.	sugar	5 mL
1 tsp.	salt	5 mL
½ tsp.	pepper	2 mL
	parsley, chopped onion or radish for garnish	

- In a large bowl, combine potatoes, eggs, celery, pepper, onion and radish.
- Blend the remaining ingredients together, except for garnishes. Pour over vegetables and mix gently.
- Garnish with parsley, chopped onion or radish. Chill.

YIELDS   **10 SERVINGS**

HINTS   *To prevent eggs from cracking while boiling, add a little salt or vinegar to the water.*

German Potato Salad

AN UNFORGETTABLE EXPERIENCE WHEN SERVED WITH PORK
OR WITH HAM AND RED CABBAGE!

6	potatoes, peeled and cubed	6
6	bacon slices	6
½ cup	chopped onion	125 mL
¼ cup	chopped celery	50 mL
1	dill pickle, chopped	1
1 tbsp.	flour	15 mL
½ cup	water	125 mL
½ cup	vinegar	125 mL
½ tsp.	sugar	2 mL
½ tsp.	salt	2 mL
¼ tsp.	dry mustard	1 mL
¼ tsp.	paprika	1 mL
1 tsp.	parsley	5 mL

- Cook potatoes in water in a saucepan until just tender. Drain and keep warm.
- In a skillet, fry bacon until crisp. Remove slices and crumble. Reserve 2 tbsp. (30 mL) of drippings.
- In reserved drippings. sauté onion, celery and pickle.
- While stirring vegetables, stir in flour. Add water, vinegar, sugar, salt and mustard. Cook on medium heat until smooth and thickened. Add crumbled bacon.
- Pour sauce over warm potatoes. Stir to distribute sauce evenly.
- Sprinkle with parsley and paprika.
- Serve warm.

YIELD   *6-8 SERVINGS*

HINTS   *Use purple onions for salads as they are milder than other types of onion and they add a new color dimension to your salad.*

CARROT SALAD

HEALTHY, COLORFUL AND TERRIFICALLY TASTY!

4 cups	grated carrots	1 L
½ cup	grated purple onion	125 mL
1 cup	seedless raisins	250 mL
½ cup	mayonnaise	125 mL
½ cup	yogurt	125 mL
¼ cup	lemon juice	50 mL
¼ tsp.	salt	1 mL

- Combine carrots, onion and raisins.
- In another bowl, mix mayonnaise, yogurt, lemon juice and salt together. Pour over carrot mixture. Mix gently. Chill and serve.

VARIATIONS *Add peeled, quartered orange slices for additional fresh flavor.*

YIELD *8 SERVINGS*

CARROT COPPER PENNY SALAD

AN EXCELLENT BUFFET DISH!

8	large carrots	8
1	onion, sliced & separated into rings	1
1	green pepper, chopped	1
10 oz.	can tomato soup	284 mL
½ cup	vegetable oil	125 mL
½ cup	sugar	125 mL
¾ cup	vinegar	175 mL
1 tsp.	prepared mustard	5 mL
1 tbsp.	Worcestershire sauce	15 mL
½ tsp.	salt	2 mL
1 tsp.	pepper	5 mL
1 tsp.	dill seed	5 mL

- Peel, slice and cook carrots until tender. Drain. Cool.
- Add onion and pepper to carrots.
- Combine the remaining ingredients. Pour over vegetables and refrigerate for 12 hours before serving.

YIELD *8 SERVINGS*

LAYERED VEGETABLE SALAD

AN ATTRACTIVE SALAD FOR A BARBECUE OR BUFFET LUNCHEON!

3 cups	shredded salad greens	750 mL
3	green onions, chopped	3
2	medium zucchini, sliced	2
2	large carrots, shredded	2
2 cups	sliced mushrooms	500 mL
1 cup	chopped celery	250 mL
2	medium tomatoes, diced	2
	shredded cheese, bacon bits, chopped green onion OR parsley for garnish	

DRESSING

1 cup	creamed cottage cheese	250 mL
½ cup	sour cream	125 mL
½ cup	plain yogurt (optional)	125 mL
¼ cup	mayonnaise	50 mL
½ tsp.	salt	2 mL
1 tsp.	mustard	5 mL
1 tbsp.	lemon juice	15 mL

- In a clear straight-sided large glass bowl, layer vegetables in order given, leave garnish suggestions until serving time.
- Combine dressing ingredients, mixing well. Spread over vegetables. Cover with clear plastic wrap. Refrigerate for 4 hours or overnight.
- To serve, garnish with shredded cheese, bacon bits, chopped green onion or parsley.
- If desired, toss salad lightly before serving.

YIELD   **8-10 SERVINGS**

LAYERED PASTA SALAD

A SPECIAL TREAT FOR THE PASTA LOVER!

3 cups	cooked pasta, shells, macaroni, etc.	750 mL
1 tbsp.	vegetable oil	15 mL
2 cups	shredded lettuce	500 mL
3	hard-boiled eggs, sliced	3
8 oz.	ham, cubed	250 g
10 oz.	frozen green peas, cooked and cooled	283 g
1 cup	shredded Monterey Jack cheese	250 g
1 cup	mayonnaise	250mL
½ cup	sour cream	125 mL
2 tsp.	Dijon mustard	10 mL
¼ cup	sliced green onions	50 mL
2 tbsp.	chopped fresh parsley	30 mL

- Toss pasta with oil.
- In a straight-sided glass bowl, layer the pasta, lettuce, eggs, ham, peas and cheese.
- Combine the mayonnaise, sour cream and mustard and then spread over the cheese.
- Sprinkle the green onions and parsley on top.
- Chill for at least 6 hours before serving. This salad may be made a day ahead and refrigerated.

YIELD   *6-8 SERVINGS*

Coleslaw

NOTHING IS TASTIER THAN A FRESH HOME-GROWN CABBAGE
MADE INTO COLESLAW!

4 cups	finely shredded cabbage	1 L
½ cup	chopped red onions	125 mL
1 cup	grated carrots	250 mL
½ cup	raisins (optional)	125 mL
1 tbsp.	sugar	15 mL
½ cup	chopped apple	125 mL
2 tbsp.	mayonnaise	30 mL
2 tbsp.	lemon juice	30 mL
½ tsp.	salt	2 mL
¼ tsp.	pepper	1 mL

- In a large mixing bowl, combine cabbage, onions, carrots and raisins. Sprinkle with sugar. Refrigerate for 1 hour.
- Add apples to cabbage mixture.
- Combine remaining ingredients. Pour over cabbage mixture and toss lightly.

YIELD   **8-10 SERVINGS**

TWO-WEEK COLESLAW

AN OLD-FASHIONED FAVORITE

1 cup	white vinegar	250 mL
1 cup	granulated sugar	250 mL
1 tsp.	celery seed	5 mL
1½ tsp.	mustard seed	7 mL
½ tsp.	turmeric	2 mL
1 tsp.	salt	5 mL
½ cup	vegetable oil	250 mL
1	medium cabbage, finely shredded	1
2	medium carrots, finely shredded	2
1	medium onion, grated	1
2	green peppers, finely chopped	2

- In a saucepan, combine vinegar, sugar, celery seed, mustard seed, turmeric and salt. Bring to a boil and continue to boil until sugar is dissolved. Cool; add oil and mix well.
- Combine vegetables in a mixing bowl. Pour cooled dressing over and mix well. Store in a large glass bowl or jar for a minimum of 24 hours before serving.
- This salad will keep well, refrigerated, for up to 2 weeks.

YIELD   *10-12 SERVINGS*

WALDORF SALAD

A FAVORITE FOR A LADIES' LUNCHEON

2 cups	diced apple	500 mL
1 cup	diced celery	250 mL
½ cup	chopped walnuts	125 mL
½ cup	raisins OR halved, seedless grapes	125 mL
½ cup	mayonnaise	125 mL
2 tsp.	lemon juice	10 mL
6-8	lettuce leaves	6-8
	paprika	

- Combine apple, celery, walnuts and raisins or grapes.
- In another bowl, mix mayonnaise with lemon juice; pour over apple mixture. Mix gently.
- On serving plates, arrange lettuce leaves into cups. Fill cups with salad. Sprinkle with paprika. Serve.

YIELD   *6-8 SERVINGS*

FRUIT SALAD

ADAPTABLE TO YOUR FAVORITE FRUITS IN SEASON!

2 cups	water	500 mL
1 cup	sugar	250 mL
¼ cup	lemon juice	50 mL
½ tsp.	salt	2 mL
2 tbsp.	ground anise	30 mL
14 oz.	can pineapple tidbits	398 mL
1 cup	of each type of chopped fruit	250 mL

- In a saucepan, combine water, sugar, lemon juice, salt and anise. Simmer for 20 minutes. Cool.
- Combine undrained pineapple with fruit. Add sauce and mix gently. Chill until ready to serve. This salad keeps well, refrigerated, in an airtight container.
  Suggested fruits: watermelon, cantaloupe, honeydew, grapes, blueberries, apples and oranges. Fruits that tend to soften, like bananas, kiwi and strawberries, should be added just prior to serving.

YIELD   *6-8 SERVINGS*

Twenty-Four Hour Fruit Salad

A PREPARE-AHEAD PLEASER THAT MAY BE SERVED AS A MAIN COURSE OR
AS A DESSERT. CHILDREN LOVE THIS LIGHT, FLUFFY CONFECTION

1	egg	1
2 tbsp.	sugar	30 mL
2 tbsp.	lemon juice	30 mL
⅛ tsp.	salt	0.5 mL
½ cup	whipping cream, whipped	125 mL
48	miniature marshmallows	48
14 oz.	can pineapple tidbits, drained	398 mL
1 cup	seedless raisins	250 mL
8	maraschino cherries, halved	8
½ cup	slivered almonds	125 mL

- In a double boiler, beat the egg. Stir in sugar, lemon juice and salt. Cook over boiling water for 5 minutes, stirring frequently. Cool.
- Fold cooled lemon mixture into whipped cream. Fold in the fruit and marshmallows.
- Refrigerate overnight.
- To serve, fold in almonds.

For larger crowds, double the amounts. Various fruits may be included, but bananas should be added just prior to serving.

YIELD   **12 SERVINGS**

FRUIT IN RUM SAUCE

A LIGHT, FRESH SALAD OR DESSERT WITH A TANGY SAUCE.

1	cantaloupe	1
1	honeydew melon	1
½	watermelon	½
1 cup	sugar	250 mL
½ cup	water	125 mL
1 tbsp.	grated lemon rind	15 mL
½ cup	lemon juice	125 mL
½ cup	light rum	125 mL
2 cups	blueberries	500 mL

- Peel and seed melons. Cut fruit into balls or chop.
- In a saucepan, combine sugar and water. Bring to a boil; reduce heat; simmer for 5 minutes. Add lemon rind; cool. Add lemon juice and rum.
- Combine melon balls with blueberries. Pour cooled liquid over fruit. Chill several hours. Serve.

YIELD   *12-16 SERVINGS*

COTTAGE CHEESE JELLIED SALAD

A SUMMER FAVORITE!

3 oz.	pkg. orange OR lemon-flavored gelatin	85 g
1 cup	boiling water	250 mL
½ cup	mayonnaise	125 mL
1 cup	cottage cheese	250 mL
1 cup	drained crushed pineapple	250 mL
½ cup	chopped walnuts	125 mL

- Dissolve gelatin in boiling water. Add mayonnaise; whisk to blend; chill until mixture just begins to set.
- Add cottage cheese, pineapple and walnuts. Combine well.
- Pour gelatin mixture into a lightly oiled 4-cup (1 L) jelly mold or a clear glass bowl. Chill.

YIELD   *6 SERVINGS*

HINTS   *Store cottage cheese and sour cream cartons upside down in the refrigerator to double the life of the contents.*

BEET HORSERADISH JELLIED SALAD

EQUALLY DELICIOUS SERVED AT A SUMMER PICNIC OR WITH ROAST BEEF!

14 oz.	can diced beets	398 mL
1 tbsp.	unflavored gelatin (1 env.)	7 g
¼ cup	cold water	50 mL
½ tsp.	salt	2 mL
¼ cup	sugar	50 mL
¼ cup	vinegar	50 mL
¾ cup	finely chopped celery	175 mL
1 tbsp.	minced onion	15 mL
1 tbsp.	horseradish	15 mL

- Drain beets. Reserve liquid. Measure reserved liquid and if necessary add water to measure ¾ cup (175 mL).
- In a saucepan, sprinkle gelatin over the ¼ cup (50 mL) cold water. Stir over low heat until gelatin dissolves. Remove from heat. Add salt, sugar and vinegar. Combine well.
- Add beet liquid to gelatin mixture, stir to combine well. Chill until mixture just begins to set.
- Add celery, onion and horseradish, mix gently.
- Pour into a lightly greased 3-cup (750 mL) jelly mold. Chill until set.
- To serve, unmold and garnish as desired.

YIELD   *6 SERVINGS*

BLUEBERRY-RHUBARB SAUCE

GREAT OVER PANCAKES OR CRÊPES!
ALSO GREAT ON ICE CREAM!

1 cup	chopped rhubarb	250 mL
1 cup	blueberries	250 mL
⅓ cup	sugar	75 mL
2 tbsp.	water	30 mL
1 tbsp.	lemon juice	15 mL

- In a saucepan, combine all ingredients. Bring to a boil. Cook over low heat for 10 minutes.
- Serve warm or cool.

VARIATIONS   *Substitute other berries or fruit for rhubarb and blueberries. Amounts may be doubled or tripled if required.*

YIELD   *1⅓ CUPS (325 mL) SAUCE*

See photograph opposite page 16.

RAISIN SAUCE

ADDS A RICH SPICY FLAVOR TO BOILED HAM

1½ cups	raisins	375 mL
2 cups	water	500 mL
1 cup	sugar	250 mL
¼ tsp.	cloves	1 mL
2 tbsp.	butter	30 mL
2 tbsp.	flour	30 mL
1 tbsp.	lemon juice	15 mL

- In a saucepan, combine raisins, water, sugar and cloves. Heat to the boiling point and boil slowly for 5 minutes.
- Melt butter, stir in flour. Add to raisin mixture while stirring constantly.
- Cook, stirring constantly, until sauce is thickened. Add lemon juice; stir. Remove from heat.
- Serve with ham.

YIELD   *2½ CUPS (625 mL)*

MUSHROOM SAUCE

A PLEASING ALTERNATIVE TO GRAVY OR USE IN RECIPES
CALLING FOR MUSHROOM SOUP

¼ cup	butter	50 mL
1 cup	sliced mushrooms	250 mL
⅓ cup	flour	75 mL
2 cups	beef broth	500 mL
½ tsp.	salt	2 mL
¼ tsp.	pepper	1 mL

- Melt butter in a skillet; sauté mushroom slices. Remove mushrooms and set aside.
- Add flour to skillet and cook until slightly browned, stirring constantly.
- Continue to stir, and add broth gradually. Cook until thickened.
- Return mushrooms to sauce. Season with salt and pepper.

YIELD   *APPROXIMATELY 2 CUPS (500 mL)*

BARBECUE SAUCE

GREAT FOR CHICKEN, GROUND BEEF OR STEAK,
ON THE BARBECUE OR IN THE OVEN!

½ cup	ketchup	125 mL
⅓ cup	vinegar	75 mL
¼ cup	brown sugar	50 mL
2 tbsp.	butter OR margarine	30 mL
2 tbsp.	Worcestershire sauce	30 mL
2 tbsp.	lemon juice	30 mL
1 tsp.	salt	5 mL
2 tsp.	chili powder	10 mL
2 tsp.	dry mustard	10 mL
1 tbsp.	finely chopped onion	15 mL
2	garlic cloves, minced (optional)	2

- In a saucepan combine all ingredients. Bring to a boil and simmer for 10 minutes. Cool. Store in refrigerator.

YIELD   *1⅓ CUPS (325 mL)*

SOUPS

Welcome to our wonderful soups.
Satisfying and hearty main course soups
need only a salad and biscuits to complete
a meal. Light and flavorful vegetable and
fruit soups add zest and flair to any
occasion. These soups are easy to prepare
and rewarding to serve.

Clam Chowder

A GREAT AFTER-SKIING, SKATING OR ICE-FISHING TREAT!

4	slices bacon, cut up	4
1	medium onion, chopped	1
1 cup	chopped celery	250 mL
10 oz.	can clams	284 mL
3 cups	cubed potatoes	750 mL
2 cups	water	500 mL
1 tsp.	salt	5 mL
½ tsp.	pepper	2 mL
¼ tsp.	thyme	1 mL
2 tbsp.	butter	30 mL
2 tbsp.	flour	30 mL
2 cups	cereal cream	500 mL

- In a large kettle, fry bacon. Pour off all but 1 tbsp. (15 mL) of bacon drippings. Add onion and celery. Sauté until tender.
- Drain clams reserving liquid. Add clam juice, potatoes, water and spices to kettle. Boil until potatoes are tender.
- Chop clams into bite-sized pieces. Add to kettle.
- Melt butter. Add flour to make a paste. Add cereal cream. Mix well. Add to kettle and bring to a boil. Simmer for 10 minutes.
- Serve hot with Cheese Bread, page 16.

YIELD   6 SERVINGS

See photograph opposite page 48.

FISH CHOWDER

A HEARTY, TASTY SOUP

1½ lbs.	white fish fillets, firm-fleshed	750 g
2 tbsp.	butter	30 mL
1 cup	chopped onion	250 mL
½ cup	diced celery	125 mL
3 cups	diced raw potatoes	750 mL
1 cup	sliced carrots	250 mL
3 cups	boiling water	750 mL
1 tsp.	salt	5 mL
¼ tsp.	pepper	1 mL
2 cups	milk	500 mL
	chopped green onions OR parsley for garnish	

- Cut fish fillets into bite-sized pieces.
- In a large heavy saucepan, melt the butter. Sauté the onion and celery in the butter until limp.
- Add the potatoes, carrots, water, salt and pepper. Simmer until vegetables are tender, about 25 minutes.
- Add the fish. Cook for another 10 minutes or until fish is cooked.
- Add the milk. Reheat but do not boil.
- To serve, garnish with chopped green onions or parsley.

YIELD   *6 SERVINGS*

WONTON SOUP

WONTONS:

1 lb.	ground pork	500 g
5 oz.	shrimp, finely chopped	140 g
¼ cup	finely chopped onion	50 mL
½ tsp.	garlic powder	2 mL
¼ tsp.	salt	1 mL
1	egg, separated	1
1 tsp.	soy sauce	5 mL
1 lb.	wonton wrappers	500 g

- In a mixing bowl, combine pork, shrimp, onion, garlic powder, salt, egg white and soy sauce. Mix well.
- Place 1 tsp. (5 mL) of pork mixture on the corner of each wonton wrapper. Roll that corner over filling and fold in each side, using egg yolk to seal folds. Do not roll up entire wrapper, allow corner opposite from where pork was placed to extend out.
- Boil wontons in a kettle of boiling water for 5 minutes. Drain well.
- Serve in wonton broth immediately or rinse with cold water, drain and freeze for use later. To freeze wontons, place on cookie sheet. When frozen, place in plastic bags and seal.

YIELD   **APPROXIMATELY 72 WONTONS**

BROTH: (For 20 wontons)

2 cups	water	500 mL
2 cups	chicken broth	500 mL
2 tbsp.	soy sauce	30 mL
20	wontons	20
1 cup	pea pods	250 mL
¼ cup	chopped green onion	50 mL

- In a saucepan, combine water, chicken broth and soy sauce and bring to a boil. Add wontons. Reduce heat and simmer for 15 minutes.
- Just prior to serving, add pea pods and green onions. Simmer for an additional 2 minutes.
- Serve immediately.
- This broth may be doubled or tripled according to servings required.

YIELD   *4 SERVINGS*

BORSCH (BEET SOUP)

A UKRAINIAN, GERMAN, POLISH AND RUSSIAN TRADITION
EVERYBODY'S FAVORITE!

4 cups	diced beets	1 L
1 cup	diced carrots	250 mL
4 cups	beef broth	1 L
4 cups	water	1 L
1	large onion, chopped	1
1	garlic clove, minced	1
1 tbsp.	lemon juice OR vinegar	15 mL
2 cups	diced potatoes	500 mL
2 cups	shredded cabbage	500 mL
2 tbsp.	finely chopped fresh dillweed	30 mL
1 tsp.	salt	5 mL
½ tsp.	pepper	2 mL
1 cup	whipping cream	250 mL

- Place beets and carrots in a large kettle with broth and water. Bring to a boil.
- Add onion, garlic and lemon juice. Simmer until beets and carrots are tender, about 30 minutes.
- Add potatoes. Continue to simmer until potatoes are tender, about 15 minutes.
- Add cabbage, dillweed, salt and pepper. Continue to simmer until cabbage is tender, about 15 minutes. Extra water may be added at this point to obtain desired consistency.
- Just prior to serving add the cream. Stir to heat. Do not boil the soup once the cream has been added or it will curdle.

NOTE	*The above ingredients serve only as a guide. They may be added to, omitted or decreased as desired. Many people add a spoonful of sour cream to each serving of Borsch.*
VARIATIONS	*The cook with limited time may wish to substitute 2 cans of cooked, diced beets for the raw beets and adjust the cooking method accordingly.*
YIELD	**8 SERVINGS**

FRENCH ONION SOUP

AN INTERNATIONAL CLASSIC

1	large onion, sliced	1
2 tbsp.	butter	30 mL
3 cups	beef broth	750 mL
¼ tsp.	salt	1 mL
⅛ tsp.	pepper	0.5 mL
2	slices French bread, toasted	2
½ cup	shredded Swiss or Gruyère cheese	125 mL

- In a skillet, sauté onion slices in butter until tender and transparent. Add broth, salt and pepper. Bring to a boil. Reduce heat and simmer for 15 minutes.
- Pour hot soup mixture into individual ovenproof dishes. Top with toasted bread. Sprinkle with cheese.
- Broil for 2-3 minutes or until cheese is melted.
- Serve immediately.

YIELD   **2 SERVINGS**

SPLIT-PEA SOUP

THE BEST WAY KNOWN TO USE UP A HAM BONE!

1	ham bone	1
8 cups	water	2 L
2 tsp.	salt	10 mL
1 tsp.	coarse black pepper	5 mL
1	bay leaf	1
2 cups	chopped onion	500 mL
1 cup	chopped celery	250 mL
1½ cups	split peas	375 mL

- In a large kettle, place ham bone, water, salt, pepper and bay leaf. Bring to a boil, cover, reduce heat, and simmer for 2 hours.
- Take bone out, remove meat from bone. Return meat to kettle.
- Add onion, celery and peas to kettle. Cover and simmer for 2 more hours or until peas are soft.

YIELD   **6-8 SERVINGS**

HINTS   *Vary the amount of salt according to the variety of ham.*

POTATO-CHEESE SOUP

SERVE WITH A TOASTED WHOLE-WHEAT SANDWICH!

1	large potato, peeled, diced	1
1 cup	water	250 mL
2 cups	beef broth	500 mL
2 cups	milk	500 mL
1 cup	light cream	250 mL
¼ cup	flour	50 mL
2 tbsp.	butter	30 mL
½ lb.	Cheddar cheese, grated	250 g
1 tbsp.	grated onion	15 mL
¼ tsp.	paprika	1 mL
1 tsp.	salt	5 mL
1 tbsp.	minced parsley	15 mL

- In a 3-quart (3 L) saucepan, cook potato in water. Drain off water. Reserve. Put cooked potato through a ricer or sieve.
- Return potato to saucepan, along with reserved potato water, beef broth, milk and cream. Heat, stirring, for 5 minutes.
- Blend flour and butter together. Add to potato mixture. Stir constantly while cooking until mixture thickens and is smooth. Boil for 2-3 minutes.
- Add cheese and onion. Reduce heat. Stir to melt cheese.
- Add seasonings and parsley.
- Serve hot.

YIELD   *4 SERVINGS*

CREAM OF MUSHROOM SOUP

VERSATILE — SERVE AS A FIRST COURSE OR USE IN YOUR FAVORITE RECIPES

1 lb.	mushrooms	500 g
2 tbsp.	butter	30 mL
4 cups	chicken broth	1 L
1 cup	finely chopped celery	250 mL
½ cup	finely chopped onion	125 mL
¼ cup	chopped parsley	50 mL
1	bay leaf, crushed	1
¼ cup	butter	50 mL
¼ cup	flour	50 mL
2 cups	light cream	500 mL

- Finely chop half of the mushrooms. Slice the other half.
- In a large skillet, sauté the mushrooms in butter. Add chicken broth, celery, onion, parsley and bay leaf. Simmer for 20 minutes.
- In a small saucepan, melt the remaining butter. Stir in flour; gradually add light cream. Cook over low heat, stirring until smooth and thick.
- Add sauce to mushroom mixture. Cook while stirring until smooth and thick.
- Serve immediately or cool and freeze in 1½ cup (375 mL) portions for use in recipes calling for a can of mushroom soup.
- When mushrooms are readily available this recipe may be doubled — serve some immediately and freeze the remainder.

YIELD   *6 CUPS (1.5 L)*

Clam Chowder, page 42
Cheese Bread, page 16

CORN-TOMATO CHOWDER

A GREAT AFTER SKIING OR SKATING TREAT WITH FRESH BISCUITS!

2 tbsp.	butter	30 mL
¼ cup	chopped onion	50 mL
¼ cup	chopped celery	50 mL
1	garlic clove, minced	1
2 tbsp.	flour	30 mL
2 cups	peeled, chopped, fresh tomatoes	500 mL
2	potatoes, diced	2
1 cup	chicken broth	250 mL
2 cups	milk	500 mL
2 cups	kernel corn	500 mL
½ tsp.	thyme	2 mL
½ tsp.	salt	2 mL
¼ tsp.	pepper	1 mL

- In a large heavy saucepan, sauté onion, celery and garlic in butter. Sprinkle with flour. Mix well.
- Add tomatoes, potatoes and broth. Bring to a boil, reduce heat and boil gently until potatoes are tender.
- In a separate saucepan heat, but do not boil, milk. Add heated milk and corn to tomato mixture. Mix well. Add seasonings. Heat, but do not boil. Serve hot.

YIELD　　*4 SERVINGS*

FRESH TOMATO SOUP

A DELICIOUS AUTUMN TREAT WHEN THERE IS AN ABUNDANCE OF FRESH TOMATOES!

2 cups	peeled and finely chopped tomatoes	500 mL
1 tsp.	baking soda	5 mL
1 cup	milk	250 mL
¼ tsp.	salt	1 mL
¼ tsp.	pepper	1 mL
1 tbsp.	parsley	15 mL

- In a saucepan, bring tomatoes to a boil. Reduce heat. Add baking soda; mix well.
- In a separate saucepan, heat milk just to the boiling point. Add to the tomato mixture. Simmer slowly until thoroughly heated (do not boil the soup once the milk has been added as it will curdle). Add spices; stir. Serve hot.

YIELD　　*2-3 SERVINGS; RECIPE IS EASILY DOUBLED OR TRIPLED.*

RHUBARB SOUP

AN UNUSUAL SUMMER GARDEN SOUP!

5 cups	chopped rhubarb	1.25 L
5 cups	chicken stock	1.25 L
2 tbsp.	chopped fresh parsley	30 mL
2 tbsp.	chopped fresh dill	30 mL
1	medium potato, finely chopped	1
1	large carrot, finely chopped	1
1	stalk celery, finely chopped	1
1	medium onion, finely chopped	1
1 cup	chopped ham	250 mL
¾ cup	half and half cream	175 mL
2 tbsp.	instant blending flour	30 mL
½ tsp.	freshly ground black pepper	2 mL

- In a soup kettle, cook rhubarb in just enough water to cover. Bring to a boil. Drain this first water off rhubarb, then add the chicken stock.
- Add the remaining ingredients, except the cream, flour and pepper. Boil slowly for approximately 1 hour or until the vegetables are tender.
- Add cream, flour and pepper. Bring just to the boiling point. Serve.

YIELD   *6-8 SERVINGS*

FRUIT SOUP

A SCANDINAVIAN CREATION THAT IS SERVED EITHER WARM OR COLD,
THIS IS EQUALLY DELICIOUS AS THE FIRST COURSE OR AS DESSERT

1 lb.	dried mixed fruit (apples, apricots, peaches, pears)	500 g
1 cup	seedless raisins	250 mL
2	cinnamon sticks	2
6 cups	water	1.5 L
1	orange	1
3 cups	pineapple juice	750 mL
⅔ cup	sugar	150 mL
3 tbsp.	tapioca	45 mL

- In a large, heavy kettle, combine the fruit, raisins, cinnamon and water. Bring to a boil; simmer for 30 minutes.
- Cut orange, with peel, into ½" (1 cm) slices.
- Add orange and remaining ingredients to kettle. Bring to a boil. Cover. Reduce heat. Cook for an additional 15 minutes over low heat.

YIELD   *6 SERVINGS*

VEGETABLES

Maintain or regain your healthy lifestyle
with these taste-tempting vegetable dishes.
Flavor and nutrition are key ingredients in
these easy-to-prepare recipes. Prove to the
reluctant vegetable eaters in your family
that healthy can also taste great!

CAULIFLOWER CASSEROLE

SECOND HELPINGS ARE PAR FOR THIS DISH

1	large head cauliflower	1
2 cups	sliced fresh mushrooms (optional)	500 mL
½ cup	chopped celery	125 mL
¼ cup	butter	50 mL
2 tbsp.	flour	30 mL
¼ tsp.	dry mustard	1 mL
½ tsp.	salt	2 mL
1¼ cup	milk	300 mL
1 cup	grated Swiss cheese	250 mL
½ cup	crushed cornflakes	125 mL

- Break cauliflower into florets. Wash and then steam for 5 minutes. Drain. Put into a greased 2-quart (2 L) ovenproof casserole.
- Sauté mushrooms and celery in butter. Blend in flour, mustard and salt. Stir well. Gradually stir in milk. Cook slowly for about 8 minutes or until thickened. Add cheese, stirring until melted. Pour sauce over the cauliflower.
- Sprinkle cornflakes crumbs on cauliflower. Bake at 350°F (180°C) for 30 minutes.

VARIATIONS *To reduce calories, use skim milk and a low-fat content cheese. Mozzarella or Cheddar may be used in place of the Swiss cheese.*

YIELD ***6 SERVINGS***

CREAMED CARROTS

A GREAT WAY TO PERK UP CARROTS IN THE WINTER!

1 lb.	carrots, pared and sliced	500 g
2 tbsp.	butter	30 mL
1	onion, chopped	1
1 tbsp.	flour	15 mL
¾ cup	chicken broth	175 mL
¼ tsp.	salt	1 mL
¼ tsp.	pepper	1 mL
½ tsp.	dillweed	2 mL
¼ cup	light cream	50 mL

- Boil carrots for 10 minutes or until tender. Drain then place in a buttered 2-quart (2 L) ovenproof casserole.
- Sauté onions in butter until transparent. Stir flour into onions. Gradually stir in chicken broth, salt, pepper and dillweed. Cook until thickened and smooth. Add cream; stir well.
- Pour sauce over carrots.
- Bake at 350°F (180°C) for 30 minutes or until thoroughly heated.
  This dish may be prepared early in the day and heated just prior to serving.

YIELD   *4-6 SERVINGS*

BROCCOLI BAKE

WHAT A PLEASANT SURPRISE FOR THOSE WHO DISLIKE BROCCOLI

6	eggs, beaten	6
16 oz.	cottage cheese	500 g
⅓ cup	flour	75 mL
¼ tsp.	salt	1 mL
½ cup	melted butter	125 mL
1½ cups	cubed Cheddar cheese	375 mL
1 lb.	broccoli, chopped	500 g

- Combine eggs and cottage cheese. Add flour, salt and butter and mix thoroughly.
- Sprinkle Cheddar cheese and broccoli into the bottom of a buttered 2-quart (2 L) ovenproof casserole. Pour cottage cheese mixture over broccoli.
- Bake at 350°F (180°C) for 30 minutes or until broccoli is tender.

YIELD   *6-8 SERVINGS*

RED CABBAGE WITH APPLES

A FLAVORFUL SWEET AND SOUR COMBINATION!

¼ cup	butter	50 mL
2 tbsp.	sugar	30 mL
1	medium onion, chopped	1
½	red cabbage, chopped	½
2	tart apples, peeled and chopped	2
2 tbsp.	vinegar	30 mL
¼ tsp.	salt	1 mL
¼ tsp.	pepper	1 mL

- In a skillet, melt butter. Add sugar and onion. Cook, stirring, until lightly browned.
- Add cabbage, apples, vinegar, salt and pepper. Cover and cook over low heat until cabbage is tender.

YIELD   *4-5 SERVINGS*

See photograph opposite page 96.

BEET LEAF ROLLS

A DELICIOUS CABBAGE ROLL VARIATION

	boiling water	
	fresh-picked beet leaves	
1 cup	rice	250 mL
2 cups	cold water	500 mL
½ tsp.	salt	2 mL
¼ cup	chopped onion	50 mL
½ cup	butter	125 mL
¼ cup	chopped fresh dillweed	50 mL
¼ tsp.	pepper	1 mL
1 cup	sour cream	250 mL
1 tsp.	chopped fresh dillweed	1 mL
1 tbsp.	finely chopped onion	15 mL

- Pour boiling water over beet leaves. Let them sit for 10 minutes or until wilted, then drain.
- In a saucepan, cook the rice in salted water until tender and fluffy.
- In a skillet, fry the onions in butter until transparent. Add the dillweed and pepper. Stir onion mixture into the rice.
- Place 1 tbsp. (15 mL) of rice mixture at the base of each beet leaf. Fold sides of leaf over filling. Roll up from base to tip of leaf.
- Place rolls in layers in a buttered 2-quart (2 L) ovenproof casserole. Pour ½ cup (125 mL) water over the beet rolls.
- Bake at 300°F (150 C) for 1 hour.
- In a saucepan, simmer sour cream, dillweed and onion. Pour over hot beet rolls just prior to serving.

VARIATIONS *Substitute cabbage leaves for beet leaves; omit the dillweed in the rice mixture and add ½ cup (125 mL) fried chopped bacon. Tomato soup, sauce or juice may replace water over the rolls during baking. Increase baking time to 2 hours or until cabbage is tender.*

YIELD *4-5 SERVINGS*

GLAZED ONIONS

RICH IN COLOR AND FLAVOR

2 lbs.	small cooking onions	1 kg
½ cup	raisins	125 mL
¼ cup	butter	50 mL
1 tbsp.	brown sugar	15 mL
1	small bay leaf, crushed	1
¼ tsp.	thyme	1 mL
¼ tsp.	salt	1 mL
⅛ tsp.	pepper	0.5 mL
3	drops of Tabasco sauce	3

- Peel onions. Cut a small cross at the root end of each. Parboil in water for 10 minutes or until just tender. Drain.
- In a large skillet over medium heat melt butter; add raisins, brown sugar and onions. Turn onions frequently to glaze them. Sprinkle with seasonings and Tabasco sauce. Stir well and serve.

SERVING
SUGGESTION *Delicious with roast chicken, pork or wild game.*

YIELD *4-6 SERVINGS*

See photograph opposite page 96.

TURNIP CASSEROLE

A TURNIP LOVER'S TREAT THAT IS ESPECIALLY GOOD WITH TURKEY!

5 cups	mashed cooked turnip	1.25 L
1 cup	chopped apples	250 mL
¼ cup	butter	50 mL
¼ cup	brown sugar	50 mL
1 tsp.	salt	5 mL
¼ tsp.	pepper	1 mL
2	eggs	2
1¾ cup	fine bread crumbs	425 mL
2 tbsp.	melted butter	30 mL

- Combine all ingredients, except bread crumbs and melted butter. Mix well and place in a buttered 2-quart (2 L) ovenproof casserole.
- Mix bread crumbs with melted butter then sprinkle on top of casserole.
- Bake, uncovered, at 350°F (180°C) for 45 minutes or until thoroughly heated.

This recipe is easily halved. It may be made ahead of time and kept refrigerated until time to heat.

YIELD   *8 SERVINGS*

POTATO PATTIES

LEFTOVER MASHED POTATOES DELUXE!

2 cups	cold mashed potatoes	500 mL
1	egg	1
½ tsp.	salt	2 mL
1 tsp.	parsley	5 mL
½ tsp.	prepared mustard	2 mL
1 tbsp.	grated onion	15 mL
1 cup	grated cheese	250 mL
1 cup	dry bread crumbs	250 mL

- Combine the first 6 ingredients, shape into patties.
- Combine grated cheese with bread crumbs
- Coat patties with crumb mixture.
- Place patties on a well-oiled cookie sheet. Bake at 375°F (190°C) for 30 minutes or until golden brown.

YIELD   *10-12 PATTIES*

POTATO PANCAKES

MIRACULOUSLY EASY AND OH SO DELICIOUS!

3	eggs	3
6	medium potatoes, grated	6
1	medium onion, grated	1
⅓ cup	flour	75 mL
¼ tsp.	baking powder	1 mL
1 tsp.	salt	5 mL
½ tsp.	pepper	2 mL
1 tsp.	chopped parsley (optional)	5 mL
½ tsp.	finely chopped dillweed (optional)	2 mL

- Lightly beat the eggs. Mix in the potatoes and onion.
- Combine flour, baking powder, salt and pepper. Add to egg mixture. Stir until just blended. Add herbs if desired.
- Drop batter in ¼ cup (50 mL) portions onto a hot skillet. When edges of pancake begin to brown, flip to brown the other side.
- Serve with sour cream or as an accompaniment to a meal.

YIELD   *6 SERVINGS*

HINTS   *Never use new potatoes for potato pancakes as they are too watery.*

ZUCCHINI TOMATO STIR-FRY

1 tbsp.	butter	15 mL
¼ cup	chopped onion	50 mL
3 cups	chopped zucchini	750 mL
¼ tsp.	salt	1 mL
¼ tsp.	basil	1 mL
¼ tsp.	pepper	1 mL
1 tbsp.	chopped parsley	15 mL
2	tomatoes, chopped	2
½ cup	grated Cheddar cheese	125 mL

- In a skillet, melt butter; add onions and sauté until transparent.
- Add zucchini, salt, basil, pepper and parsley. Stir-fry until zucchini is tender.
- Add the tomatoes, stir for an additional 2 minutes.
- Sprinkle cheese on top. Cover briefly, until cheese is melted.
- Serve hot.

YIELD   *6 SERVINGS*

ZUCCHINI PANCAKES

THESE DELECTABLE PANCAKES ARE A PERFECT WAY TO USE UP ZUCCHINI AND CARROTS.

2 cups	grated zucchini	500 mL
1 cup	grated carrots	250 mL
½ cup	grated onion	125 mL
2	eggs	2
1 tsp.	salt	5 mL
1 tsp.	baking powder	5 mL
1 tsp.	chopped parsley	5 mL
½ tsp.	pepper	2 mL
1 cup	flour	250 mL

- In a mixing bowl, combine all ingredients.
- For each pancake, pour a large spoonful of batter onto a hot skillet. Brown on both sides for 2-3 minutes. Serve hot.

YIELD   *12 PANCAKES*

HINTS   *To prevent pancakes from sticking, rub the cut side of a raw potato over the griddle.*

STUFFED TOMATOES

COLORFUL, FLAVORFUL AND EASY TO MAKE!

3	large tomatoes	3
⅓ cup	butter	75 mL
3 cups	fresh bread crumbs	750 mL
1	medium onion, chopped	1
1 tsp.	basil	5 mL
10 oz.	pkg. spinach, cooked, drained, chopped	283 g
¼ lb.	grated Cheddar cheese	125 g
3 tbsp.	grated Parmesan cheese	45 mL

- Cut tomatoes in half horizontally. Scoop out the insides leaving a shell. Invert on paper toweling to drain.
- In skillet, melt butter. Stir in crumbs, onion and basil, cooking until lightly browned.
- Set aside ¼ cup (50 mL) of crumb mixture for topping.
- Combine the spinach and Cheddar cheese with the remaining crumb mixture.
- Fill tomato halves with spinach-crumb mixture. Place in a buttered baking dish. Bake at 350°F (180°C) for 20 minutes or until heated thoroughly.
- Remove from oven and sprinkle tops with reserved crumbs and Parmesan cheese. Return to oven and bake for 5 minutes or until tops are lightly browned and cheese is melted.

VARIATIONS   *In place of spinach, use scooped out tomato pieces.*

YIELD   *6 SERVINGS*

PRESERVES & PICKLES

Enhance your meals with fresh-tasting flavor from your garden. Homemade pickles, sauces and salsa have a superb flavor that commerical varieties never match. Your own salsa, pickles and marmalade also makes a great gift!

TOMATO SAUCE

WHAT A WAY TO PRESERVE THAT FRESH TOMATO TASTE FOR COOKING LATER IN THE YEAR!

4 qts.	chopped skinned tomatoes	4 L
3	large onions, chopped	3
4	celery stalks, chopped	4
4	carrots, chopped	4
3	green peppers, chopped	3

- In a large kettle combine all vegetables. Bring to a gentle boil, cook until vegetables are just tender. Drain off juice.
- Process small portions of vegetables in a blender.
- Return blended vegetables to kettle and simmer for 1 hour. Cool.
- Refrigerate for immediate use or freeze in smaller portions for use in chili, spaghetti sauce and other favorite recipes. Season as desired and according to dish in which it is to be used.
- For small portions for soups and stews, freeze in ice cube trays. When solid, transfer cubes to freezer containers.

YIELD   **APPROXIMATELY 12 CUPS**

SALSA

ESPECIALLY FOR THOSE WHO LIKE IT HOT!

6 cups	chopped, peeled tomatoes	1.5 L
2	sweet green peppers, chopped	2
2	sweet red peppers, chopped	2
12	hot peppers, chopped	12
2	medium onions, chopped	2
2	garlic cloves, chopped	2
½ cup	sugar	125 mL
½ tsp.	salt	2 mL
2 cups	cider vinegar	500 mL

- In a large heavy saucepan, combine all ingredients. Bring to a boil. Reduce heat. Cook on medium heat, stirring occasionally, for 1 hour or until slightly thickened. Cool.
- Refrigerate for 1 month or freeze in smaller portions.
- Serve with tacos or as an accompaniment with eggs or grilled meat dishes.

YIELD   **6 CUPS**

See photograph opposite page 64.

ANTIPASTO

A WONDERFUL APPETIZER TO KEEP ON HAND

½ cup	vegetable oil	125 mL
4	green peppers, chopped	4
6 cups	drained, chopped mixed sweet pickles (reserve juice)	1.5 L
2 x 10 oz.	cans drained, sliced mushrooms	2 x 284 mL
2 x 8 oz.	cans drained, sliced waterchestnuts	2 x 227 mL
1	head cauliflower, chopped	1
1 cup	chopped pimientos	250 mL
1½ cups	drained, chopped green stuffed olives	375 mL
4 cups	ketchup	1 L
2 x 10 oz.	jars hot chili sauce	2 x 285 mL
4 x 6.5 oz.	cans drained water-packed tuna	4 x 184 mL
5	bay leaves	5
2 tbsp.	cinnamon	30 mL
5	cloves	5

- In a large heavy pan, heat oil. Sauté all chopped and sliced vegetables for 3 minutes.
- Add ketchup and chili sauce to vegetables. Use ½ cup (125 mL) drained pickle juice to rinse out bottles. Add to vegetables.
- Add tuna, bay leaves and spices.
- Simmer, stirring continuously for 10 minutes.
- Remove bay leaves. Remove from heat, set to cool. Bottle and seal with a hot water bath or place in containers and freeze. Store for 1 week before using, to allow flavors to ripen.
- Serve with your favorite crackers.

YIELD   *APPROXIMATELY 12 PINT (500 mL) JARS*

See photograph opposite page 64.

HINTS   *To peel tomatoes, plunge into boiling water for 45 seconds, dip into ice water and skins will be easy to remove.*

DILL PICKLES

DILLS — JUST LIKE THOSE FROM GRANDMA'S CROCK!

12 cups	water	3 L
1 cup	vinegar	250 mL
½ cup	salt	125 mL
	sprigs of fresh dill	
	garlic cloves	
	pickling cucumbers	

- In a large kettle, combine water, vinegar and salt and bring to a boil.
- Place 2 garlic cloves and a sprig of dill in the bottom of each sterlized jar. Pack jars with cucumbers. Cover cucumbers with hot brine. Seal jars.
- In a canner bring water to a boil. Turn off heat. Place jars in canner with water level above the lids. Let sit for 20 minutes or until the cucumbers change color. Pickles are ready to use in 2 weeks.

NOTE *The above method of sealing the jars prevents the pickles from getting overly sour.*

YIELD *4 QUARTS (4 L)*

See photograph opposite.

Pickles and Preserves (left to right)
Salsa, page 62
Sweet Cucumber Pickles, page 67
Dill Pickles, page 64
Antipasto, page 63
Beet Pickles, page 68
Christmas Pepper Jelly, page 164
Carrot Marmalade, page 68

BREAD AND BUTTER PICKLES

CRISP, SWEET AND SPICY

4 qts.	sliced cucumbers	4 L
12	medium onions, sliced	12
3	sweet red peppers, chopped	3
3	green peppers, chopped	3
½ cup	pickling salt	125 mL
6 cups	white sugar	1.5 L
5 cups	vinegar	1.25 L
2 tsp.	mustard seed	10 mL
1 tsp.	celery seed	5 mL
2 tsp.	turmeric	10 mL
1 tbsp.	allspice	15 mL

- Place cucumbers, onions and peppers in a large bowl. Sprinkle with pickling salt. Let stand overnight.
- The next day, squeeze out the liquid from the vegetables.
- In a large kettle, combine sugar and vinegar. Tie the spices in a bag and place in the brine. Simmer for 10 minutes. Add the vegetables. Boil for 5 minutes.
- Pack in sterilized jars and seal. Pickles are ready to use in 1 week.

YIELD *8 PINT (500 mL) JARS*

HINTS *A convenient method of sealing jars is to heat the oven to 250°F (120°C). Turn off oven. Place packed jars in oven. Leave in closed oven until cool.*

ALREADY CUT PICKLES

SERVING-SIZE PICKLES WITH GREAT FLAVOR

½ cup	pickling salt	125 mL
10 cups	boiling water	2.5 L
4 lbs.	cucumbers, cut lengthwise in sticks	2 kg
3 cups	vinegar	750 mL
1 cup	water	250 mL
2 cups	sugar	500 mL
1 tsp.	dry mustard	5 mL
1 tsp.	celery seed	5 mL
1 tsp.	mustard seed	5 mL
1 tsp.	turmeric	5 mL

- In a glass bowl, dissolve the salt in the water. Add the cucumber sticks. Let stand overnight.
- The next day, in a large kettle, combine the remaining ingredients and bring to a boil.
- Drain the cucumber sticks and add to the boiling vinegar mixture. Bring to the boiling point again.
- Pack cucumber sticks and brine in sterilized jars and seal.

YIELD   ***ABOUT 6 PINT (500 mL) JARS***

SWEET CUCUMBER PICKLES

A GREAT PICKLE THAT CAN BE MADE FROM "NOT SO PERFECT" CUCUMBERS!

5 lbs.	cucumbers	2.2. kg
2	large onions, sliced	2
1 tsp.	turmeric	5 mL
2 tsp.	pickling spice	10 mL
2 cups	water	500 mL
2 cups	vinegar	500 mL
3 cups	sugar	750 mL
¼ cup	pickling salt	50 mL

- Wash the cucumbers. Cut into bite-sized pieces.
- Place a slice of onion in the bottom of each pint (500 mL) sealer jar. Place cucumber pieces on top.
- In a large saucepan, combine the remaining ingredients. Bring to a boil, turn down heat and continue to simmer for 10 minutes.
- Pour hot brine over cucumbers in jars. Seal with rubber rings or snap on lids. Place in an oven that has been preheated to 250°F (120°C). Turn oven off, but leave jars in until the oven cools. (This seals the jars the same way that a hot water bath does).

YIELD   *APPROXIMATELY 6 PINT (500 mL) JARS*

See photograph opposite page 64.

BEET PICKLES

1 qt.	vinegar	1 L
2 qts.	water	2 L
2 cups	sugar	500 mL
3 tbsp.	pickling spice	45 mL
4 qts.	peeled cooked beets	4 L

- In a large kettle, combine vinegar, water and sugar.
- Place pickling spice in a bag and put in kettle. Bring liquids and spice to a boil, simmer for 15 minutes.
- Slice beets into pint (500 mL) jars. Add ½ tsp. (2 mL) pickling salt to each jar. Pour hot brine over beets. Seal immediately.
- Process in boiling water bath for 10 minutes.

YIELD   ***8 PINT (500 mL) JARS***

See photograph opposite page 64.

CARROT MARMALADE

CARROTS PLUS CITRUS — SUPERB!

8 cups	grated carrots	2 L
2	lemons	2
2	oranges	2
5 cups	sugar	1.25 L

- In a large kettle, cook carrots in as little water as possible. Drain, reserve the liquid. Return carrots to kettle.
- Cut rind from lemons and oranges. Chop rind finely. Discard pits and membranes. Chop fruit pulp finely.
- Add rind, pulp and sugar to carrots. Add 1 cup (250 mL) of reserved liquid.
- Bring to a full rolling boil while stirring constantly. Reduce heat and continue to cook for 45 minutes or until thick.
- While hot, pour marmalade into hot sterilized jars and seal.

YIELD   ***4 PINT (500 mL) JARS***

See photograph opposite page 64.

HINTS   *A piece of cheesecloth or the clean toe of a nylon stocking makes a perfect bag in which to hold the spices.*

MAIN COURSES

Treat yourself and your family to these comforting, often familiar flavors. North American, European and Eastern main-dish favorites are presented in an easy-to-follow style with suggested variations to pique your imagination. Here is comfort food at its finest!

ROULADEN

THANKS TO THE GERMAN PEOPLE FOR SHARING THIS SPECIAL TREAT!

6	rouladen*	6
1 tsp.	prepared mustard per rouladen	5 mL
2	large onions, sliced	2
6	slices of bacon	6
6	dill pickle slices	6
	salt & pepper to taste	
1 tbsp.	vegetable oil	15 mL
1 cup	water OR beef broth	250 mL
1 tbsp.	cornstarch	15 mL
2 tbsp.	water	30 mL

- Lay meat pieces flat. Spread each with mustard.
- Divide onion slices among meat slices. Lay onions on meat along with a slice of bacon and a slice of dill pickle. Season with salt and pepper. Carefully roll up each piece of meat with filling inside. Fasten with a toothpick or tie with string.
- Brown rolls in oil. Place in a 2-quart (2 L) ovenproof casserole.
- Add water to drippings. Pour over the rolls and cover.
- Bake at 300°F (150°C) for 2 hours or until meat is tender.
- Remove rouladen from casserole. Dissolve cornstarch in water. Stir into pan juices until thickened. Serve hot.

* 3 x 4" (7 x 10 cm) thin rectangles of pounded flank, round or sirloin steak.

YIELD   4 SERVINGS

PEPPER STEAK

A QUICK, EASY AND HEALTHY DISH WITH CHINESE ORIGINS

¼ cup	soy sauce	50 mL
1 tbsp.	water	15 mL
1 ½ tsp.	cornstarch	7 mL
¼ tsp.	pepper	1 mL
2	garlic cloves, minced	2
1 lb.	round steak, thinly sliced	500 g
2 tbsp.	butter OR margarine	30 mL
2	green peppers, diced	2
2	tomatoes, cut into wedges	2
1 cup	sliced mushrooms	250 mL

- Blend together the soy sauce, water, cornstarch, pepper and garlic. Pour over steak in a shallow pan and let marinate for a minimum of 1 hour.
- Melt butter in a large skillet. Add meat and soy sauce mixture. Cook until meat looses its red color or for about 4-5 minutes.
- Add the peppers and cook for 1 minute.
- Add the tomatoes and mushrooms. Cook for 2-3 minutes longer.
- Serve immediately on steamed white rice.

YIELD   *3-4 SERVINGS*

BEEF STEW

COMFORT FOOD AT ITS BEST!

¼ cup	flour	50 mL
1 tsp.	salt	5 mL
½ tsp.	pepper	2 mL
1 ½ lbs.	cubed stewing beef	750 g
¼ cup	vegetable oil	50 mL
2	medium onions, sliced	2
1	garlic clove, minced	1
12 oz.	beer (1 bottle)	340 mL
1 tbsp.	soy sauce	15 mL
1 tbsp.	Worcestershire sauce	15 mL
½ tsp.	thyme	2 mL
2	bay leaves	2
2 cups	tomato juice	500 mL
2 cups	water	500 mL
4	carrots, peeled and sliced	4
½	turnip, peeled and cubed	½
4	parsnips, peeled and sliced	4
3	potatoes, peeled and diced	3
	flour & water for thickening	

- In a plastic bag, combine flour, salt and pepper. Drop cubed beef into bag and shake to dredge cubes.
- In a large heavy saucepan, heat oil. Add beef cubes to brown. Add onion and garlic; cook until onions are transparent.
- Add beer, soy sauce, Worcestershire sauce, thyme, bay leaves, tomato juice and water. Bring to a boil. Reduce heat and simmer, covered, for 2 hours.
- Add carrots, turnip, parsnips and potatoes. Continue to simmer until all vegetables are tender, about 1 hour. Remove bay leaves. Thicken with flour and water.
- Serve with Parsley Dumplings, page 73.

NOTE *The above vegetables serve only as a guide. They may be added to, omitted, or decreased as desired.*

VARIATIONS *This recipe may be prepared using a crock pot or baked slowly in the oven. These methods will require additional cooking time.*

YIELD *6 SERVINGS*

PARSLEY DUMPLINGS
LIGHT, FLUFFY AND TENDER

1	egg	1
½ cup	water	125 mL
1 cup	flour	250 mL
2 tsp.	baking powder	10 mL
½ tsp.	salt	2 mL
1 tbsp.	finely chopped parsley	15 mL

- Beat egg and water together.
- Combine flour, baking powder, salt and parsley. Add to egg mixture. Combine lightly.
- Drop batter by tablespoons (15 mL) on top of hot, cooked stew. Cover and let steam for 10 minutes. Serve hot with stew.

YIELD   **8 LARGE DUMPLINGS**

OLD-FASHIONED SHEPHERD'S PIE
A GREAT CASSEROLE DISH MADE FROM SUNDAY DINNER'S LEFTOVERS

2 cups	diced cooked roast beef	500 mL
1 cup	chopped cooked vegetables	250 mL
½ cup	chopped onion	125 mL
½ cup	chopped celery	125 mL
2 cups	gravy	500 mL
½ tsp.	salt	2 mL
¼ tsp.	pepper	1 mL
2 cups	cooked mashed potato	500 mL

- Combine roast, vegetables, onion and celery. Place in a 2-quart (2 L) buttered oven-proof casserole.
- In a saucepan, heat gravy. Pour over roast mixture. Sprinkle with salt and pepper.
- Spread mashed potatoes over gravy.
- Bake at 325°F (160°C) for 1 hour or until thoroughly heated.
- These amounts are easily varied according to the amount of leftovers.

YIELD   **4 SERVINGS**

HINTS   *To prepare chopped parsley, cut with a pair of sharp scissors.*

HASH BROWN STROGANOFF PIE

A ONE-DISH MEAL — EASY AND GOOD

2 cups	hash brown potatoes	500 mL
1	egg	1
1 tbsp.	sour cream	15 mL
1 lb.	lean ground beef	500 g
½ cup	chopped onion	125 mL
¼ cup	chopped celery	50 mL
1 cup	mushroom sauce, page 40 OR mushroom soup, page 48	250 mL
¼ cup	sour cream	50 mL
¼ tsp.	salt	1 mL
¼ tsp.	pepper	1 mL
1 cup	grated Cheddar cheese	250 mL

- Combine the potatoes, egg and sour cream. Press into a greased 8" (20 cm) pie plate. Bake at 350°F (180°C) for 15 minutes.
- In a skillet, brown the beef. Drain off excess fat. Add the onion and celery. Sauté until onions are transparent. Add soup, sour cream, salt and pepper. Mix well. Spread beef mixture in hash brown shell. Top with grated cheese.
- Bake at 350°F (180°C) for 30 minutes.
- Serve with a tossed salad and a vegetable dish.

YIELD   **4 SERVINGS**

GROUND BEEF ROLLS

NOT TO BE CONFUSED WITH UKRAINIAN CABBAGE ROLLS
BUT EQUALLY AS GOOD

1	cabbage	1
1 lb.	ground beef	500 g
1 cup	cooked rice	250 mL
½ cup	chopped onion	125 mL
1 tsp.	salt	5 mL
½ tsp.	pepper	2 mL
½ tsp.	poultry seasoning	2 mL
¼ tsp.	thyme	1 mL
1	egg	1
	oil for frying	

SAUCE:

1 cup	tomato sauce, page 62	250 mL
1 tbsp.	brown sugar	15 mL
¼ cup	water	50 mL
1 tbsp.	vinegar	15 mL

- Remove core from the cabbage. Blanch the cabbage head by putting it in a large pot of boiling water. Boil for 5 minutes or until leaves are soft and separate easily. Separate leaves and place in cold water to cool. Cut out the core from the leaves to make them easier to roll. Do not cut the leaves; use the whole leaf.
- In a mixing bowl combine the beef, rice, onion, seasonings and egg.
- Place a tablespoon (15 mL) of beef mixture at the base of each leaf. Fold sides in and roll up leaf. Fasten with a toothpick. Brown each roll lightly in hot oil. Place in a buttered 2-quart (2 L) ovenproof casserole.
- Combine sauce ingredients. Mix well. Pour sauce over beef rolls.
- Bake at 325°F (160°C) for 1½ hours or until cabbage is tender.

YIELD　　　*6 SERVINGS*

GROUND BEEF LOAF

A TASTY LOAF SERVED PIPING HOT, BUT ALSO GREAT SLICED
FOR SANDWICHES THE NEXT DAY

⅔ cup	milk	150 mL
3	slices dry bread, cubed	3
1 lb.	ground beef	500 g
2	eggs	2
1	medium onion, chopped	1
1 tsp.	salt	5 mL
¼ tsp.	pepper	1 mL
½ cup	grated Cheddar cheese	125 mL
¼ cup	brown sugar	50 mL
¼ cup	ketchup	50 mL
1 tbsp.	prepared mustard	15 mL

- Add milk to bread and soak for a few minutes.
- In a mixing bowl, combine soaked bread with beef, eggs, onion, salt, pepper and cheese.
- Place beef mixture in a 5 x 9" (13 x 23 cm) loaf pan.
- Combine brown sugar, ketchup and mustard. Spread evenly over the loaf.
- Bake at 350°F (180°C) for 1 hour.

YIELD   *4 SERVINGS*

CHILI CON CARNE

GREAT TO COME HOME TO AFTER A WINTER DAY OUTDOORS!

2 tbsp.	vegetable oil	30 mL
1 ½ lbs.	lean ground beef	750 g
1 cup	chopped onion	250 mL
2	garlic cloves, minced	2
2 cups	stewed tomatoes	500 mL
1 cup	tomato sauce, page 62	250 mL
1 cup	sliced mushrooms	250 mL
2 x 14 oz.	cans kidney beans	2 x 398 mL
14 oz.	can pork and beans	398 mL
2 tbsp.	chili powder	30 mL
1 tbsp.	hot chili or pepper sauce	15 mL
1 tsp.	black pepper	5 mL
1 tsp.	oregano	5 mL

- Heat oil in a large heavy pan; sauté beef, onion and garlic until beef is no longer pink.
- Add remaining ingredients. Simmer for 3 hours, stirring occasionally.
- Serve hot with Pepper Corn Bread, page 15 or Biscuits, page 13.

YIELD   **8-10 SERVINGS**

See photograph opposite page 80.

MEATBALLS
ENOUGH VARIETIES TO SATISFY EVERYONE!

2 lbs.	lean ground beef	1 kg
1 cup	bread crumbs	250 mL
¼ cup	milk	50 mL
1	egg	1
1 tsp.	salt	5 mL
½ tsp.	pepper	2 mL
½ tsp.	garlic powder	2 mL
½ tsp.	onion powder	2 mL

- Combine all ingredients. Mix well. Roll into 1" (2.5 cm) balls.
- Place on broiler pan and broil for 10-15 minutes, turning occasionally.
- Serve with any of the sauces which follow or with Spaghetti Sauce, page 103.

YIELD   *6-8 SERVINGS*

BARBECUE SAUCE FOR MEATBALLS

2 cups	tomato sauce, page 62	500 mL
½ cup	water	125 mL
¼ cup	vinegar	50 mL
¼ cup	brown sugar	50 mL
2 tbsp.	prepared mustard	30 mL
2 tbsp.	Worcestershire sauce	30 mL
½ cup	chopped onion	125 mL

- In a saucepan, combine the above ingredients. Bring to a boil. Reduce heat and simmer for 15 minutes.
- Pour sauce over prepared meatballs in an ovenproof casserole. Heat at 350°F (180°C) for 30 minutes or until thoroughly heated.

ONION SAUCE FOR MEATBALLS

¼ cup	butter	50 mL
4	large onions, chopped	4
¼ cup	flour	50 mL
½ tsp.	salt	2 mL
¼ tsp.	pepper	1 mL
1 cup	chicken broth	250 mL
¾ cup	milk	175 mL
1 cup	grated Cheddar OR Parmesan cheese	250 mL

- In a large skillet melt butter; add onions and sauté until transparent.
- Sprinkle flour, salt and pepper over onions. Stir well to blend.
- Add chicken broth and milk slowly, while stirring constantly. Cook until thickened.
- Stir in ½ of the cheese. Mix well. Pour sauce over prepared meatballs in an ovenproof casserole. Sprinkle with the remaining cheese.
- Bake at 350°F (180°C) for 30 minutes or until thoroughly heated.

PINEAPPLE SAUCE FOR MEATBALLS

2 tbsp.	cornstarch	30 mL
1 cup	brown sugar	250 mL
2 x 14 oz.	cans pineapple tidbits, drained, reserve syrup	2 x 398 mL
2 tbsp.	soy sauce	30 mL
⅔ cup	vinegar	150 mL
½ cup	chopped green pepper	125 mL

- Mix cornstarch with sugar. Add reserved pineapple syrup, soy sauce and vinegar. Cook over low heat, stirring, until smooth and thick. Simmer for 2 minutes. Add pineapple tidbits and green pepper.
- Pour sauce over prepared meatballs in an ovenproof casserole.
- Bake at 350°F (180°C) for 30 minutes or until thoroughly heated.

CANNELLONI

ONE OF ITALY'S MOST POPULAR STUFFED PASTAS

24	cannelloni shells *	24
1 tbsp.	butter	15 mL
½ cup	minced onions	125 mL
1 lb.	lean ground beef OR veal	500 g
20 oz.	spinach, chopped and squeezed dry	600 g
1 cup	cottage cheese	250 mL
2	eggs	2
½ tsp.	nutmeg	2 mL
½ tsp.	salt	2 mL
¼ tsp.	pepper	1 mL
2 cups	spaghetti sauce, page 103 **	500 mL
½ cup	Parmesan cheese	125 mL

- Cook cannelloni as per package directions, until soft.
- In a skillet, melt butter; add onion and sauté until transparent. Add the meat and continue to cook until the liquid has cooked away. Remove from heat.
- To meat, add spinach, cottage cheese, eggs, nutmeg, salt and pepper. Mix well.
- Stuff a heaping tablespoon of meat mixture into each shell. In a lightly greased 9 x 13" (23 x 32 cm) baking dish spread a thin layer of spaghetti sauce. Arrange filled shells over sauce. Pour remaining spaghetti sauce over cannelloni. Sprinkle with Parmesan cheese. Cover with foil.
- Bake at 350°F (180°C) for 45 minutes. Uncover and continue to cook for an additional 15 minutes.

* If you get frustrated with the shells or tubes — you can use cannelloni sheets which roll up like crêpes.

** If you are pressed for time a commercial spaghetti sauce may be used.

YIELD   **6-8 SERVINGS**

Chili, page 77
Pepper Corn Bread, page 15

LASAGNA

ITALIAN COMFORT FOOD. MAKE 2 AND FREEZE ONE FOR EMERGENCIES

12 oz.	lasagna noodles	350 g
1 1 /2 lbs.	ground beef	750 g
1 cup	chopped onion	250 mL
28 oz.	canned tomatoes	796 mL
14 oz.	can tomato sauce	398 mL
2	garlic cloves, minced	2
1 ½ tsp.	oregano	7 mL
1 tsp.	crushed basil	5 mL
2 cups	creamed cottage cheese	500 mL
1	egg	1
½ cup	Parmesan cheese	125 mL
12 oz.	mozzarella cheese slices	350 g

- Cook noodles. Rinse well. Set aside.
- In a skillet, brown beef. Pour off grease; add chopped onion and brown until transparent. Add tomatoes, tomato sauce, garlic, oregano, and basil. Simmer for 15 minutes. Set aside.
- In a separate bowl, combine cottage cheese, egg, and Parmesan cheese.
- On the bottom of a lightly greased 9 x 13" (23 x 32 cm) baking dish, place a layer of noodles. Layer with half of the meat mixture, another layer of noodles, cottage cheese mixture, another layer of noodles and the other half of meat mixture. Top with a layer of noodles. Place cheese slices on top. Cover with foil.
- Bake at 375°F (190°C) for 45 minutes. Uncover and continue to bake for another 15 minutes.

VARIATIONS　　*For spinach lasagna, 10 oz. (280 g) chopped spinach may be added to the cottage cheese mixture.*

YIELD　　*6-8 SERVINGS. THIS RECIPE FREEZES WELL.*

HINTS　　*To prevent noodles or rice from boiling over or sticking together, add a few drops of vegetable oil to the water.*

VEAL CORDON BLEU

FROM FRANCE'S FAMED COOKING SCHOOL — SIMPLE AND SAVORY

4	veal cutlets	4
4	thin slices ham	4
4	slices Swiss cheese	4
2 tbsp.	flour	30 mL
½ tsp.	salt	2 mL
¼ tsp.	pepper	1 mL
¼ tsp.	allspice	1 mL
1	egg, beaten	1
½ cup	dry bread crumbs	125 mL
¼ cup	vegetable oil	50 mL
2 tbsp.	water	30 mL

- Pound cutlets to ¼" (1 cm) thickness.
- Place a slice of ham and a slice of cheese on each cutlet. Roll up cutlets, secure with a toothpick.
- Combine flour and spices. Mix well. Coat each cutlet roll in seasoned flour. Dip rolls in beaten egg and roll in bread crumbs.
- Heat oil in a deep skillet, brown rolls on all sides. Add water, cover, and simmer for 45 minutes.
- Transfer cutlets to a shallow baking pan. Bake, uncovered, at 350°F (180°C) for 15 minutes or until crispy.

YIELD   *4 SERVINGS*

MARINATED PORK ROAST

PREPARE ONE DAY — RELAX AND ENJOY THE NEXT!

¼ cup	honey	50 mL
3 tbsp.	brown sugar	45 mL
¼ cup	water	50 mL
⅓ cup	ketchup	75 mL
2 tbsp.	soy sauce	30 mL
2 tsp.	paprika	10 mL
1 tsp.	dry mustard	5 mL
¼ tsp.	ginger	1 mL
3 lbs.	pork roast	1.5 kg

- To prepare marinade, combine all ingredients, except roast, in a saucepan. Bring to a boil. Cool.
- Marinate roast overnight in refrigerator.
- The next day, remove roast from marinade and place in a shallow roasting pan.
- Roast at 350°F (180°C) for 35 minutes on 1 side. Turn over and bake an additional 1½ hours. Baste with marinade while roasting.
- This roast may also be done on the barbecue, on a spit or in a shallow baking pan.

YIELD   **6 SERVINGS**

See photograph opposite page 96.

HONEY PORK CHOPS
PREPARE EARLY IN THE DAY OR EVEN THE NIGHT BEFORE!

6-8	pork chops	6-8
½ cup	honey	125 mL
¼ cup	cider vinegar	50 mL
2 tbsp.	soy sauce	30 mL
2 tbsp.	chopped crystallized ginger	30 mL
1	garlic clove, minced	1
½ tsp.	ground pepper	2 mL

- Place pork chops in a shallow baking dish.
- Combine the remaining ingredients. Pour over pork chops. Refrigerate for 8 hours or overnight, turning chops occasionally.
- Bake at 350°F (180°C) for 1 hour or until chops are tender. Turn chops frequently during baking time.
- Serve on rice.

VARIATIONS   *Try this marinade with chicken or ham. It is delicious.*

YIELD   *6 SERVINGS*

PORK CHOPS AND RICE

A HEARTY MEAL IN 1 POT

1 tbsp.	vegetable oil	15 mL
6	pork chops	6
1	medium onion, chopped	1
¼ cup	chopped green pepper	50 mL
1 cup	raw rice	250 mL
½ tsp.	salt	2 mL
¼ tsp.	pepper	1 mL
2 cups	beef broth	500 mL
1 tbsp.	Worcestershire sauce	30 mL
2	tomatoes, sliced	2

- In a skillet, heat oil, brown pork chops. Place 3 chops in the bottom of a 2-quart (2 L) ovenproof casserole. Set the other 3 chops aside.
- Sauté onion and pepper in pork chop drippings.
- Place raw rice on top of pork chops in casserole. Place onion and pepper on top of rice. Sprinkle with salt and pepper. Cover with the remaining 3 chops.
- Combine the beef broth with the Worcestershire sauce. Pour over chops and rice in casserole.
- Place tomato slices on top.
- Bake, covered, at 350°F (180°C) for 1 hour or until rice is tender.

YIELD *4 SERVINGS*

SPARERIBS IN SAUCE

A NO-FUSS METHOD FOR TENDER, SPICY RIBS

3 lbs.	lean pork spareribs	1.5 kg
¾ cup	brown sugar	175 mL
½ cup	ketchup	125 mL
½ cup	white vinegar	125 mL
2 tbsp.	Worcestershire sauce	30 mL
1 tsp.	chili powder	5 mL
¾ cup	water	175 mL
1	onion, chopped	1

- Trim visible fat from spareribs. Place ribs in a baking pan. Bake at 350°F (180°C) for 45 minutes. Pour off grease.
- Combine the remaining ingredients. Pour over ribs.
- Bake, turning meat occasionally, at 350°F (180°C) for 1½ hours or until meat is tender.

YIELD   *4-5 SERVINGS*

CHINESE SWEET 'N' SOUR RIBS

DEEP-FRYING MAKES THESE CRISP AND TASTY

1 tbsp.	soy sauce	15 mL
1 tsp.	vinegar	5 mL
2 lbs.	sweet 'n' sour-cut pork spareribs	1 kg
2 tbsp.	flour	30 mL
	oil for deep frying	

SWEET 'N' SOUR SAUCE

1 cup	brown sugar	250 mL
1 cup	vinegar	250 mL
2 cups	water	500 mL
2 tsp.	soy sauce	10 mL
2 tbsp.	cornstarch	30 mL
¼ cup	water	50 mL

- Combine soy sauce and vinegar. Sprinkle over ribs to moisten. Dip ribs in flour. Heat oil to 365°F (185°C). Deep-fry ribs for 5 minutes or until golden brown.
- Place ribs in a baking pan.
- To prepare sauce, in a saucepan, combine brown sugar, vinegar, water and soy sauce. Bring to a boil.
- Combine cornstarch with remaining water. Mix until smooth. Add to sugar mixture. Simmer, stirring until thick and smooth. Pour over prepared spareribs.
- Bake at 350°F (180°C) for 1 hour.

YIELD   3-4 SERVINGS

POTATO - HAM SCALLOP

A RICH CHEDDAR FLAVOR

1 tbsp.	flour	15 mL
2 tsp.	salt	10 mL
¼ tsp.	pepper	1 mL
4-6	medium potatoes, washed, pared and thinly sliced	4-6
1 cup	diced, cooked ham	250 mL
¾ cup	shredded Cheddar cheese	175 mL
½ cup	finely chopped onion	125 mL
3 tbsp.	butter OR margarine	45 mL
1 ¾ cups	scalded milk	425 mL

- Grease a shallow 6-cup (1.6 L) ovenproof casserole.
- Combine the flour, salt and pepper in a plastic bag.
- Place potato slices in bag and shake to coat.
- Layer ½ of the potatoes, ½ of the ham, ½ of the cheese and ½ of the onion in the casserole. Repeat the layers.
- Add butter to scalded milk. Pour over vegetables in casserole.
- Bake, uncovered, at 350°F (180°C) for 1¼ hours or until potatoes are tender when pierced with a fork. Turn off heat. Cover and leave in oven about 10 more minutes to absorb the liquid.
- Serve warm.

YIELD   *4-6 SERVINGS*

LIMA BEAN - SAUSAGE CASSEROLE

BAKED BEANS WITH FLAIR AND FLAVOR

2 cups	dried lima beans	500 mL
	salt	
	water	
16	link sausages	16
1 ½ cups	chopped onion	375 mL
½ cup	chopped green pepper	125 mL
1 cup	tomato sauce, page 62	250 mL
1 tbsp.	brown sugar	15 mL
1 tbsp.	molasses	15 mL
2 tsp.	salt	10 mL
½ tsp.	pepper	2 mL
½ tsp.	dry mustard	2 mL
½ cup	grated Cheddar cheese	125 mL

- Cook lima beans in boiling salted water for 2 hours or until tender. Drain.
- In a skillet, brown sausages lightly. Remove sausages and drain off all but 2 tbsp. (30 mL) of fat.
- Add onion and green pepper to reserved fat in skillet. Cook until just tender.
- To vegetables, add tomato sauce, sugar, molasses, salt, pepper, mustard and lima beans. Pour into a greased 2-quart (2 L) baking dish. Arrange sausages on top. Sprinkle with cheese.
- Bake at 350°F (180°C) for 30 minutes or until thoroughly heated.

YIELD   *6-8 SERVINGS*

STUFFED CHICKEN BREASTS
AN IMPRESSIVE PRESENTATION FOR FAMILY OR GUESTS

2 tbsp.	butter OR margarine	30 mL
¼ cup	chopped onion	50 mL
¼ cup	chopped celery	50 mL
1 tbsp.	parsley	15 mL
2 cups	fine bread crumbs	500 mL
½ tsp.	salt	2 mL
¼ tsp.	pepper	1 mL
1 tbsp.	thyme	15 mL
½ cup	chopped walnuts (optional)	125 mL
4	whole chicken breasts (8 halves)	4
2 tbsp.	melted butter OR margarine	30 mL
1 tbsp.	lemon juice	15 mL

- In a skillet, melt butter and sauté onions, celery and parsley. Add the bread crumbs, salt, pepper, and thyme; stir in the nuts.
- Add enough water to moisten the crumbs so that the dressing clings together.
- Divide crumb mixture into 4 parts and make 4 mounds. Place mounds on foil on a cookie sheet.
- Spread chicken breasts open and place on top of dressing mounds.
- Combine melted butter and lemon juice. Brush over chicken breasts.
- Bake at 350°F (180°C) for 1 hour or until chicken is tender.

VARIATIONS   *For smaller servings, halve chicken breasts and divided stuffing into 8 mounds, top stuffing with half of chicken breast. OR, do a combination of whole and halved chicken breasts.*

YIELD   ***4 SERVINGS***

CHICKEN PAPRIKA

(Paprikas Csirke)

THIS TRADITIONAL HUNGARIAN DISH FREES THE COOK
TO ENJOY THE GUESTS

¼ cup	butter OR margarine	50 mL
1	large onion, chopped	1
1	garlic clove, minced	1
1 tbsp.	Hungarian paprika	15 mL
½ tsp.	salt	2 mL
½ tsp.	pepper	2 mL
3 lbs.	chicken pieces	1.5 kg
2 cups	chicken broth	500 mL
2 tsp.	flour	10 mL
1 cup	sour cream	250 mL

- In a large skillet or heavy saucepan, heat the butter; sauté the onion and garlic in butter until golden brown. Stir in the paprika, salt and pepper. Cook for 1 minute.
- Add the chicken pieces and fry until lightly browned.
- Stir in broth. Cook over low heat for 1 hour or until chicken is tender.
- Whisk flour into sour cream. Add to chicken liquid and heat but do not boil.
- Serve with dumplings or noodles.

VARIATIONS *Vegetables such as skinned chopped tomatoes, chopped green peppers or sliced carrots may be added along with the broth.*

Cheaper, less tender cuts of meat may be substituted for the chicken. Boneless meat should be in small cubes.

YIELD ***5-6 SERVINGS***

HINTS *To crush garlic, put cloves between waxed paper or in a plastic bag and crush with a meat mallet or other heavy object. This eliminates clean-up.*

CHICKEN AND EGG NOODLES

ALTHOUGH TIME CONSUMING THIS IS WELL WORTH THE TIME AND EFFORT!

CHICKEN:

1	chicken, cut into serving pieces	1
	water	
½ cup	chopped onion	125 mL
1 tbsp.	parsley	15 mL
1 tsp.	salt	5 mL
½ tsp.	pepper	2 mL
½ cup	chopped celery	125 mL

NOODLES:

4	eggs, beaten	4
2 tbsp.	water	30 mL
1 tbsp.	oil	15 mL
3 cups	flour	750 mL
1 tsp.	salt	5 mL

- Place chicken pieces in soup kettle. Add water until chicken is completely covered. Add remaining ingredients. Simmer for 2 hours or until chicken is well done. (Meanwhile prepare noodles). Remove chicken from broth to a casserole to keep warm. Reserve broth for noodles.
- To prepare noodles, beat eggs, water and oil. Add flour and salt. Knead until flour is blended in and dough does not stick to the hands. Cover dough with a bowl and let rest for 30 minutes.
- Take pieces of dough, roll out onto a floured surface until paper thin. Sprinkle flour over each rolled out piece and stack sheets of dough. When all dough has been rolled, floured and stacked, cut dough into spaghetti-thin strips. Use adequate flour to ensure that noodles do not stick together.
- Boil the chicken broth. Add the noodles by handfuls, stirring constantly to prevent the noodles from sticking together. Additional boiling water may have to be added at this point to provide enough liquid to cook the noodles.
- When all the noodles are in the broth, turn the heat down to medium. Cook for 15 minutes, stirring frequently. The noodles will thicken the broth mixture. Serve immediately with chicken.

YIELD   **6 SERVINGS**

CRANBERRY CHICKEN

A SWEET, TART, SPICY FLAVOR THAT YOU WILL LOVE

½ cup	flour	125 mL
½ tsp.	salt	2 mL
¼ tsp.	pepper	1 mL
1	frying chicken, cut up	1
2 tbsp.	oil for frying (more if needed)	30 mL
2 cups	cranberry sauce, page 172	500 mL
⅛ tsp.	Tabasco sauce	0.5 mL
½ cup	chopped onion	125 mL
2 tbsp.	Worcestershire sauce	30 mL
½ tsp.	garlic powder (optional)	2 mL

- Combine flour, salt and pepper in a bag. Add chicken pieces and shake to coat evenly. Heat oil in a skillet, brown chicken pieces.
- Combine the remaining ingredients and place in a 2-quart (2 L) ovenproof casserole. Add the browned chicken to the sauce.
- Bake at 350°F (180°C) for 1 hour or until tender. Turn chicken frequently during baking.

YIELD **6 SERVINGS**

CHICKEN — SPINACH CASSEROLE

CHICKEN FLORENTINE FOR FAMILY AND GUESTS

10 oz.	pkg. chopped frozen spinach, thawed, drained and squeezed dry	284 mL
2	boneless chicken breasts, chopped	2
2 tbsp.	butter OR margarine	30 mL
½ tsp.	salt	2 mL
¼ tsp.	pepper	1 mL
1 tbsp.	butter	15 mL
2 cups	sliced fresh mushrooms	500 mL
1 tbsp.	flour	15 mL
1 cup	chicken broth	250 mL
½ tsp.	pepper	2 mL
¼ cup	mayonnaise	50 mL
1 tsp.	lemon juice	5 mL
⅓ cup	grated cheese	75 mL
⅓ cup	crushed cornflakes OR branflakes	75 mL

- Spread spinach in the bottom of a buttered 6-cup (1.5 L) ovenproof casserole.
- Melt butter in a skillet, add chopped chicken, sauté until lightly browned. Season with salt and pepper. Place chicken on top of spinach.
- Add remaining butter to skillet, sauté the mushrooms. When liquid begins to form, add the flour. Stir in chicken broth, stirring until thickened. Add pepper, mayonnaise and lemon juice. Pour over chicken.
- Sprinkle the chicken with cheese and crushed cereal flakes.
- Bake at 350°F (180°C) for 50 minutes.

VARIATIONS *Other less expensive chicken pieces may be boned and used in place of breasts, try thighs, drumsticks and breasts in combination.*

YIELD *4 SERVINGS*

BARBECUED CHICKEN
A WONDERFUL AROMA AND FLAVOR

¾ cup	ketchup	175 mL
1 cup	brown sugar	250 mL
¼ cup	vinegar	50 mL
1 tsp.	dry mustard	5 mL
1 tsp.	paprika	5 mL
1 tsp.	salt	5 mL
1 tsp.	pepper	5 mL
1 tsp.	garlic powder	5 mL
1 tsp.	curry powder (optional)	5 mL
3 tbsp.	Worcestershire sauce	45 mL
1	cut-up frying chicken	1

- Combine all the ingredients, except chicken, in a large, deep frying pan. Simmer for 5 minutes.
- Add the chicken (skinned if preferred). Baste the chicken in the sauce. Cook at a low temperature, turning chicken pieces occasionally, for 45 minutes or until chicken is tender.

YIELD   *4 SERVINGS*

CHICKEN WINGS

A FAVORITE APPETIZER OR MAIN COURSE THAT IS PREPARED A DAY IN ADVANCE!

3 lbs.	chicken wings	1.5 kg
¾ cup	soy sauce	175 mL
¼ cup	vinegar	50 mL
¼ cup	water	50 mL
2	garlic cloves, minced	2
1	large onion, finely chopped	1
⅓ cup	sugar	75 mL
⅓ cup	butter OR margarine	75 mL
1 ½ tsp.	dry mustard	7 mL
1 tsp.	ground ginger	5 mL
¼ tsp.	pepper	1 mL

- Cut tips off wings, discard or see hint below. Cut remaining wings in 2 parts at the joint. Place in a single layer in a glass baking dish.
- In a saucepan, combine the remaining ingredients. Bring to a boil. Cool.
- Pour sauce over wings. Marinate in refrigerator overnight.
- Bake wings in marinade at 300°F (150°C) for 2 hours.
- Serve wings warm, in sauce, over rice, or remove wings from sauce, cool and serve cold.

YIELD   **APPROXIMATELY 32 PIECES**

HINTS   *Cook chicken wing tips in lightly salted water to make chicken broth. Broth may be frozen for future use.*

FISH FILLETS IN LEMON SAUCE

EVEN NON-FISH EATERS WILL ENJOY THIS ONE!

2 lbs.	fish fillets	1 kg
¼ cup	butter	50 mL
2 cups	chopped mushrooms	500 mL
¼ cup	chopped green onion	50 mL
2 tbsp.	flour	30 mL
1 tsp.	salt	5 mL
¼ tsp.	pepper	1 mL
2 tsp.	parsley flakes	10 mL
1 tsp.	lemon peel	5 mL
1 cup	milk	250 mL

- Place fillets in a greased baking dish.
- In a skillet, melt butter, add mushrooms and onion, sauté. Stir in the remaining ingredients, cook slowly to make a thickened sauce.
- Spoon sauce over the fish.
- Bake at 350°F (180°C) for 30 minutes or until fish flakes easily.

SERVING
SUGGESTIONS *Serve with lemon-flavoured rice, cooked in chicken stock with 1 tsp. (5 mL) grated lemon peel added. Top with chopped green onion for flavor and color.*

YIELD *4 SERVINGS*

BAKED SNAPPER

A FISH LOVER'S DELIGHT!

¼ cup	butter	50 mL
1 cup	chopped onion	250 mL
½ cup	chopped celery	125 mL
1	tomato, finely diced	1
1 cup	sliced mushrooms	250 mL
1	garlic clove, minced	1
2 tbsp.	chopped parsley	30 mL
1 tsp.	basil	5 mL
¼ tsp.	paprika	1 mL
½ tsp.	salt	2 mL
¼ tsp.	pepper	1 mL
2 tbsp.	lemon juice	30 mL
1 ½ lbs.	snapper fillets	750 kg

- In a skillet, melt butter, add all ingredients except the fillets. Sauté until vegetables are tender.
- Place fish in a greased 8 x 12" (20 x 30 cm) baking dish. Pour seasoned vegetables over fish.
- Bake at 350°F (180°C) for 30 minutes or until fish flakes easily when tested with a fork. For the first half of the baking time cover with foil. Remove foil and continue to bake for remaining time.

VARIATIONS   *Substitute cod fish for snapper.*

YIELD   *4 SERVINGS*

COQUILLE ST JACQUES

SERVE — AND LISTEN TO THE RAVES! A SUPERRB APPETIZER OR MAIN COURSE

1 lb.	scallops	500 g
½ cup	water	125 mL
½ cup	dry white wine	125 mL
2	green onions, chopped	2
2	celery tops, chopped	2
2	sprigs parsley, chopped	2
1	bay leaf	1
4	peppercorns	4
¼ tsp.	thyme	1 mL
½ tsp.	salt	2 mL
¼ cup	chopped onion	50 mL
¼ cup	sliced fresh mushrooms	50 mL
¼ cup	butter	50 mL
2 tbsp.	flour	30 mL
½ cup	cream	125 mL
1	egg yolk	1
1 tbsp.	lemon juice	15 mL
¼ cup	fine bread crumbs	50 mL
2 tbsp.	grated Cheddar cheese	30 mL

- Wash, drain, and pat dry scallops.
- In a large skillet, combine and bring to a boil, water, wine, onions, celery, parsley, bay leaf, peppercorns, thyme and salt. Add scallops and simmer for 5 minutes. Remove from heat. Drain scallops; reserve broth. Set aside.
- In skillet, sauté onion and mushrooms in butter. Blend in flour. Slowly add reserved broth. Stir, while cooking slowly, until sauce is thickened.
- Mix cream with egg yolk. Add to sauce. Fold in scallop mixture and lemon juice. Mix gently. Pour into 4 lightly greased scallop shells.
- Bake at 450°F (230°C) for 8 minutes.
- Combine bread crumbs with cheese. Sprinkle over the 4 shells. Return to the oven. Broil for 2 minutes. Serve immediately.

VARIATIONS *Use an equivalent amount of filleted perch or pickerel in place of scallops. Cut fillets into bite-sized pieces.*

YIELD *4 SERVINGS*

SEAFOOD CASSEROLE

A TASTY DELIGHT FOR SEAFOOD LOVERS AND IT'S MADE IN ADVANCE!

1 cup	shell macaroni	250 mL
1 ½ cups	sliced mushrooms	375 mL
2 tbsp.	butter	30 mL
1 ½ cups	cream of mushroom soup, page 48	375 mL
1 cup	milk	250 mL
1 cup	grated Cheddar cheese	250 mL
2	hard-boiled eggs, chopped	2
1 cup	chopped crabmeat	250 mL
1 cup	broken shrimp	250 mL

- Cook macaroni in lightly salted boiling water for 5 minutes. Drain.
- Sauté mushrooms in butter.
- Combine macaroni, mushrooms and remaining ingredients. Place in a 6-cup (1.6 L) buttered ovenproof casserole. Refrigerate for 8 hours or overnight.
- Bake at 350°F (180°C) for 1 hour or until thoroughly heated.

YIELD   **6 SERVINGS**

CRAB - ZUCCHINI CASSEROLE

COLORFUL AND GRATIFYING — COMPLEMENT WITH A TOSSED GREEN SALAD

½ cup	butter	125 mL
4 cups	sliced zucchini	1 L
½ cup	chopped purple onion	125 mL
2	garlic cloves, chopped	2
1 ½ cups	chopped cooked crabmeat	375 mL
1 ½ cups	cubed Swiss cheese	375 mL
1 cup	cubed fresh bread	250 mL
3	tomatoes, cubed	3
1 tsp.	basil	5 mL
½ tsp.	salt	2 mL
¼ tsp.	pepper	1 mL

- In a skillet, melt butter, sauté zucchini and onion. Combine with the remaining ingredients.
- Place in a greased 2-quart (2 L) ovenproof casserole. Bake at 350°F (180°C) for 45 minutes.

YIELD   **4 SERVINGS**

MUSHROOM CUTLETS

A MOCK VEAL CUTLET THAT IS A REGULARLY REQUESTED DISH!

2 cups	dry bread crumbs	500 mL
½ cup	milk OR water	125 mL
1 lb.	mushrooms, chopped	500 g
1 cup	chopped onion	250 mL
3	eggs	3
1 tbsp.	parsley	15 mL
½ tsp.	salt	2 mL
¼ tsp.	pepper	1 mL

- Soak crumbs in milk. Add remaining ingredients and mix well.
- Pour ¼ cup (50 mL) portions of the mixture on a hot griddle to make pancakes. Brown evenly on both sides.
- Serve hot.

SERVING SUGGESTIONS   *Serve with Mushroom Sauce, page 40, and Stuffed Tomatoes, page 60, for a delicious vegetarian meal.*

YIELD   ***APPROXIMATELY 12 — 4" (10 cm) PANCAKES***

BAKED BEANS

A GREAT CROWD PLEASER!

2 cups	white navy beans	500 mL
5 cups	hot water	1.25 L
1 tsp.	salt	5 mL
1	onion, chopped	1
½ lb.	bacon, cut into chunks	250 g
¼ cup	brown sugar	50 mL
¼ cup	molasses	50 mL
1 tsp.	dry mustard	5 mL
¼ cup	ketchup	50 mL

- Wash and pick over beans. Place beans, water, salt, onion and bacon in a slow cooker. Mix well. Cover, plug in cooker, and cook on low heat overnight or until beans are tender.
- Drain liquid off the beans. Reserve liquid.
- Add remaining ingredients to beans. Mix well. Add reserved liquid as desired. Cover and continue to cook for an additional 2 hours before serving.

VARIATIONS *In a large ovenproof dish, soak beans overnight in water. Next morning add remaining ingredients. Mix well. Bake in a 300°F (150°C) oven for 3 to 4 hours or until tender. Before serving, remove 1 cup (250 mL) of baked beans; mash and return to dish. Serve.*

YIELD ***8 SERVINGS***

SPAGHETTI SAUCE

VERSATILE — USE IN YOUR FAVORITE RECIPES

2 tbsp.	shortening	30 mL
1	onion, chopped	1
1	garlic clove, minced	1
¼ cup	chopped celery	50 mL
5 ½ oz.	tomato paste	156 mL
2 cups	fresh chopped tomatoes OR canned	500 mL
1 tsp.	salt	5 mL
2 tsp.	sugar	10 mL
½ tsp.	pepper	2 mL
¼ tsp.	allspice	1 mL
¼ tsp.	chili powder	1 mL
¼ tsp.	thyme	1 mL
2 tbsp.	chopped parsley	30 mL
1	bay leaf	1
1-2 cups	tomato juice	250-500 mL

- In a large heavy saucepan, melt the shortening; add onion, garlic and celery and fry until onion is transparent.
- Add the remaining ingredients and simmer for 1 hour.
- Remove the bay leaf.
- Add tomato juice until sauce reaches desired consistency.
- Serve with spaghetti and meatballs.

VARIATIONS *To make a tasty meat sauce, add ½ lb. (250 g) lean ground beef to onions. Sauté until no red remains in beef.*

YIELD *3-4 SERVINGS: SAUCE TO ACCOMPANY A 6 OZ. (170 g) PKG. OF SPAGHETTI AND ½ LB. (¼ KG) OF GROUND BEEF MADE INTO MEATBALLS.*

PARMESAN CHEESE SAUCE WITH PASTA AND VEGETABLES

INTERESTING CASSEROLES ARE CREATED WITH THIS
PICK-YOUR-OWN PASTA AND VEGETABLES RECIPE!

¼ cup	butter	50 mL
2 tbsp.	flour	30 mL
1 cup	milk	250 mL
½ cup	sour cream	125 mL
½ cup	grated Parmesan cheese	125 mL
¼ cup	chopped onion (optional)	50 mL
1 tsp.	salt	5 mL
½ tsp.	pepper	2 mL
¼ tsp.	cayenne pepper	1 mL
½ tsp.	nutmeg	2 mL
3 cups	cut-up vegetables *	750 mL
1 cup	uncooked pasta, shells, macaroni, etc.	250 mL

- In a saucepan, melt the butter. Stir in the flour. Add the milk and mix well. Cook over low heat until thick. Add sour cream, cheese, onion and spices. Mix well and keep warm.
- Cook vegetables until tender, crisp in boiling salted water. Drain. Keep warm.
- Cook pasta. Drain. Keep warm.
- In a greased ovenproof casserole, combine pasta and vegetables. Pour the hot sauce over; toss. Serve immediately or place in a 350°F (180°C) oven to heat thoroughly.

* Suggested vegetables are broccoli florets, sliced mushrooms, carrots, green onions, red peppers, snow peas, asparagus, etc.

VARIATIONS *Substitute grated Swiss cheese for the Parmesan cheese and omit the nutmeg. Chopped cooked meat or shrimp or crab may also be added to make a complete 1-dish meal.*

YIELD ***4 SERVINGS***

GNOCCHI

A PASTA LOVER'S DELIGHT!

½ cup	milk	125 mL
⅓ cup	butter	75 mL
1 cup	flour	250 mL
2	eggs	2
1 tsp.	salt	5 mL
¼ tsp.	paprika	1 mL
1 ½ cups	cooked mashed potatoes	375 mL
2 tbsp.	butter	30 mL
3 tbsp.	grated cheese	45 mL

- In a saucepan, combine milk and butter. Heat to the boiling point. Stir in flour until the resulting dough forms a ball. Remove from heat.
- Beat in eggs, salt, paprika and mashed potatoes. Put dough in refrigerator to chill for 1-2 hours.
- Sprinkle flour over the dough to make it easier to handle. Roll dough into ½" (1 cm) thick cylindrical shapes. Cut into 1" (2.5 cm) long pieces. Drop dough pieces into simmering salted water. Simmer for 5 minutes. Drain.
- Place boiled gnocchi in a greased pan. Pat with butter and sprinkle with cheese. Place gnocchi in a 375°F (190°C) oven, briefly, until butter and cheese are melted.

VARIATIONS   *Serve with Tomato Sauce, page 62, OR Spaghetti Sauce, page 103.*

YIELD   *4-6 SERVINGS*

PYROHY

A UKRAINIAN DISH THAT HAS BECOME A FAVORITE OF ALL!

2 ½ cups	flour	625 mL
½ tsp.	salt	2 mL
1	egg, beaten	1
2 tbsp.	vegetable oil	30 mL
¾ cup	warm water	175 mL
¼ cup	butter, shortening OR bacon fat	50 mL
½ cup	chopped onion	125 mL

- In a mixing bowl, combine flour and salt.
- Combine egg, oil and water. Add to flour. Mix well. Knead on a lightly floured surface until dough is smooth.
- Cover dough and let "rest" for 20 minutes in a warm place.
- Roll out dough ¼" (1 cm) thick on a lightly floured surface. Cut into circles using the floured rim of a drinking glass.
- Place a teaspoonful (5 mL) of filling (see below and on page 107) in the center of each circle. Fold edges together. Pinch edges together with floured fingers to seal well.
- Drop pyrohy (about a dozen at a time) into boiling salted water. Boil for 8 minutes. Remove from water with a slotted spoon.
- Toss cooked pyrohy with butter, shortening or bacon fat in which ½ cup (125 mL) of chopped onion has been fried.
- Serve hot as is or with sour cream and fried bacon bits.

YIELD   *4 DOZEN*

CHEDDAR CHEESE/POTATO PYROHY FILLING

½ cup	chopped onions	125 mL
2 tbsp.	butter OR margarine	30 mL
2 cups	cooked mashed potatoes	500 mL
1 cup	grated Cheddar cheese	250 mL
½ tsp.	salt	2 mL
¼ tsp.	pepper	1 mL

- Sauté onions in butter until transparent. Combine with remaining ingredients. Mix well. Chill.

Cottage Cheese Pyrohy Filling

½ cup	chopped onions	125 mL
2 tbsp.	butter OR margarine	30 mL
2 cups	dry cottage cheese	500 mL
1	egg	1
½ tsp.	salt	2 mL
¼ tsp.	pepper	1 mL
1 tbsp.	finely chopped dill (optional)	15 mL

- Sauté onions in margarine until transparent. Combine with remaining ingredients. Mix well. Chill.

Sauerkraut Pyrohy Filling

½ cup	chopped onions	125 mL
2 tbsp.	butter OR margarine	30 mL
2 cups	sauerkraut	500 mL
1 cup	cooked mashed potatoes	250 mL
¼ tsp.	pepper	1 mL

- Sauté onions in butter until transparent. Combine with remaining ingredients. Mix well. Chill.

HINTS   *When making pyrohy make sure that the filling is well chilled and that filling does not get near the edges or the seal will not be secure.*

Cornmeal "Nachynka" Casserole

A GREAT DISH SERVED BY UKRAINIANS FOR SUNDAY DINNERS
AND OF COURSE AT EVERY WEDDING!

1 cup	chopped onion	250 mL
½ cup	butter	125 mL
1 cup	cornmeal	250 mL
1 tsp.	salt	5 mL
1 tsp.	sugar	5 mL
¼ tsp.	pepper	1 mL
3 ½ cups	milk	875 mL
½ cup	light cream	125 mL
3	eggs, beaten	3

- In a large skillet, fry onions in butter until transparent. Add cornmeal, salt, sugar and pepper. Mix well. Cook for 10 minutes.
- Scald milk. Gradually stir milk into the cornmeal mixture and continue stirring until all lumps disappear. Cook until thick.
- Blend in cream and eggs. Mix well.
- Place in a 2-quart (2 L) buttered ovenproof casserole. Bake at 350°F (180°C) for 1 hour.

YIELD   *6-8 SERVINGS*

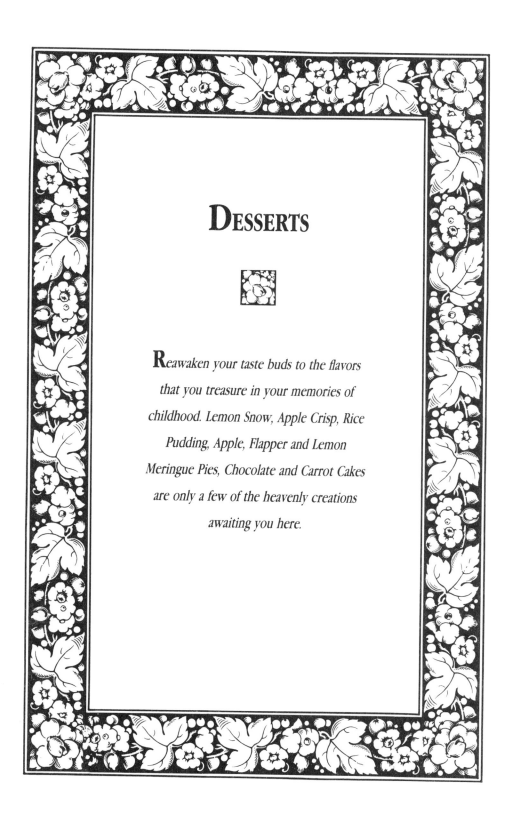

DESSERTS

Reawaken your taste buds to the flavors
that you treasure in your memories of
childhood. Lemon Snow, Apple Crisp, Rice
Pudding, Apple, Flapper and Lemon
Meringue Pies, Chocolate and Carrot Cakes
are only a few of the heavenly creations
awaiting you here.

CHEESECAKE - BASIC

A DESSERT WITH GREAT VARIATIONS!

1 cup	flour	250 mL
½ cup	butter	125 mL
¼ cup	sugar	50 mL
½ cup	finely chopped nuts	125 mL
8 oz.	cream cheese	250 g
1	egg	1
¼ cup	sugar	50 mL
1 tsp.	vanilla	5 mL
½ cup	whipping cream, whipped	125 mL
2 cups	crushed, sweetened berries OR fruit whipped cream for garnish	500 mL

- Combine flour, butter, sugar and nuts. Press into a greased 9 x 13" (23 x 32 cm) pan. Bake at 350°F (180°C) for 15 minutes. Cool.
- Beat the cream cheese with egg until light and fluffy. Add sugar and vanilla. Fold in the whipped cream. Spread on top of cooled base and refrigerate.
- Before serving, top with 2 cups (500 mL) of sauce prepared from crushed sweetened berries or fruit in season or if you are in a hurry use your favorite pie filling.
- Garnish with additional whipped cream, if desired.

VARIATIONS   *For a liqueur-flavored cheesecake, add 2 tbsp. (30 mL) of your favorite liqueur to the batter. Try Amaretto liqueur and use almonds for the crust. Also, add Amaretto to the whipped cream for garnishing. Try Peach Schnapps in the batter and top the cheesecake with sweetened sliced peaches flavored with Peach Schnapps. Apricots and Apricot Brandy would also be a sensational flavor combination — your imagination is the only limit!*

YIELD   ***10-12 SERVINGS***

APPLE CHEESECAKE

A SIMPLE BUT ELEGANT BAKED CHEESECAKE!

1 cup	flour	250 mL
⅓ cup	butter	75 mL
⅓ cup	sugar	75 mL
½ tsp.	vanilla	2 mL
8 oz.	cream cheese	250 g
1	egg	1
½ tsp.	vanilla	2 mL
⅓ cup	sugar	75 mL
2½ cups	chopped apples	625 mL
½ cup	sugar	125 mL
½ tsp.	nutmeg	2 mL
2 tbsp.	lemon juice	30 mL
1 cup	sliced almonds	250 mL

- Combine flour, butter, sugar and vanilla. Mix until crumbly then press mixture into a 10" (25 cm) springform pan.
- Beat cream cheese, egg, vanilla and sugar until creamy. Spread over crust.
- Combine apples, sugar, nutmeg and lemon juice in a heavy saucepan. Simmer gently until apples are tender, about 20 minutes.
- Spread apple filling over cheese mixture. Top with almonds.
- Bake at 425°F (220°C) for 10 minutes. Reduce heat to 350°F (180°C), bake for an additional 25 minutes.

VARIATIONS   *Try chopped peaches or pears instead of apples. Use apple pie filling or your favorite fruit filling if you are in a hurry.*

YIELD   **10 SERVINGS**

BROWNIE MOUSSE DESSERT
THE ULTIMATE TREAT FOR BROWNIE LOVERS!

1 cup	sugar	250 mL
2	eggs	2
½ cup	vegetable oil	125 mL
¾ cup	flour	175 mL
1 tsp.	baking powder	5 mL
¼ cup	cocoa	50 mL
¼ tsp.	salt	1 mL
1 cup	semisweet chocolate chips	250 mL
½ cup	chopped nuts	125 mL
8 oz.	cream cheese	250 g
½ cup	whipping cream, whipped	125 mL
1 tsp.	almond flavoring	5 mL
2 tbsp.	icing sugar	30 mL
¼ cup	toasted sliced almonds	50 mL
	almonds or shaved chocolate curls for garnish	

- In a mixing bowl, beat sugar, eggs and oil until fluffy.
- Combine flour, baking powder, cocoa and salt. Add to egg mixture, blending well.
- Stir in chocolate chips and nuts.
- Pour batter into a greased 9" (23 cm) springform pan.
- Bake at 350°F (180°C) for 25 minutes. Cool and then remove from pan.
- Beat cream cheese with whipped cream. Add almond flavoring and icing sugar. Spread on top of cooled base. Decorate with almonds or shaved chocolate curls.
- Refrigerate for at least 3 hours before serving.

YIELD   *12-16 SERVINGS*

See photograph opposite.

Brownie Mousse Dessert, page 112

ICE CREAM APPLE PIE

A REFRESHING VERSION OF APPLE PIE À LA MODE!

CRUST:

1	egg	1
¾ cup	sugar	175 mL
⅛ tsp.	salt	0.5 mL
1½ tsp.	baking powder	7 mL
½ tsp.	cinnamon	2 mL
¼ cup	flour	50 mL
½ cup	chopped apples	125 mL
½ cup	chopped walnuts	125 mL

FILLING:

1½ quarts	vanilla ice cream	1.5 L
3	chocolate-nut bars, crushed OR chopped	3

- Combine egg, sugar, salt, baking powder, cinnamon and flour. Beat well. Stir in apples and walnuts.
- Pour into a well greased 10" (25 cm) springform pan. Bake crust at 350°F (180°C) for 25 minutes (during baking crust will rise considerably but will fall later). Cool.
- Soften ice cream. Put on top of cooled crust. Top with crushed chocolate bars. Freeze.
- Remove from freezer a few minutes before serving.

VARIATIONS   *Substitute maple walnut or Dutch apple pie ice cream for the vanilla ice cream.*

YIELD   *10-12 SERVINGS*

LEMON MOUSSE

A LIGHT, TART DESSERT

1 tbsp.	unflavored gelatin (7 g pkg.)	15 mL
¼ cup	lukewarm water	50 mL
4	large eggs, separated	4
½ cup	fresh lemon juice	125 mL
1 tbsp.	grated lemon rind	15 mL
¾ cup	sugar	175 mL
1 cup	whipping cream, whipped	250 mL

- Dissolve gelatin in water. Set aside.
- Place egg yolks, lemon juice, rind, and ½ cup (125 mL) of sugar in the top of a double boiler. Cook slowly over low heat until the mixture thickens enough to coat the back of a spoon. Remove from heat.
- Add gelatin mexture to lemon mixture. Stir until gelatin is completely dissolved. Cool for 1 hour.
- Beat egg whites until stiff. Gradually add the remaining ¼ cup (50 mL) of sugar and continue to beat until very stiff peaks form. Gently fold lemon mixture into egg whites. Fold in whipped cream.
- Pour into a clear glass serving bowl or into individual serving dishes.
- Chill. To serve garnish with a twist of lemon.

This dessert may be made in advance and frozen. Remove from freezer to refrigerator a few hours prior to serving.

VARIATIONS *Line the bottom of a lightly oiled 10" (25 cm) springform pan with a crumb crust made from 1 cup (250 mL) vanilla wafer crumbs and ¼ cup (50 mL) melted butter. Pour lemon mousse over crust. Chill to set.*

YIELD ***10-12 SERVINGS***

HINTS *Mousse desserts look elegant when served in stemmed glassware.*

LEMON SOUFFLÉ

A LIGHT, ELEGANT FINALE — PERFECT FOR A DINNER OR LUNCHEON!

2 tbsp.	unflavored gelatin (2 x 7 g pkg.)	30 mL
½ cup	water	125 mL
6	eggs	6
1½ cups	sugar	375 mL
1 tbsp.	grated lemon rind	15 mL
⅔ cup	fresh lemon juice	150 mL
1 cup	whipping cream, whipped	250 mL
½ cup	whipping cream, whipped (optional)	125 mL

- Wrap foil around the top of a soufflé dish to make a 2" (5 cm) collar. Tie or tape in place.
- In a small saucepan, sprinkle gelatin over water. Let stand for 10 minutes or until soft. Melt over low heat.
- In a large mixing bowl, combine eggs and sugar. Beat at high speed until light, about 8 minutes.
- Add lemon rind and juice to gelatin mixture. Pour into egg mixture. Continue to beat until well blended. Chill for 5 minutes.
- Gently fold whipped cream into egg mixture until no white streaks are visible.
- Pour into soufflé dish and refrigerate.
- Remove foil collar before serving.
- If desired, before serving, garnish by piping additional whipped cream on top, using a pastry bag fitted with a wide tip.

YIELD   *10-12 SERVINGS*

HINTS   *Soaking lemons and other citrus fruits in hot water for a few minutes yields more juice or try microwaving on HIGH for 30-45 seconds.*

LEMON SNOW

AN OLD-FASHIONED FAVORITE!

1 tbsp.	unflavored gelatin (7 g pkg.)	15 mL
¼ cup	cold water	50 mL
¾ cup	hot water	175 mL
½ cup	sugar	125 mL
¼ cup	lemon juice	50 mL
1 tbsp.	grated lemon rind	15 mL
2	egg whites, stiffly beaten	2

- Soak gelatin in cold water for 10 minutes.
- Dissolve sugar in hot water.
- Pour hot mixture over softened gelatin. Stir well to completely dissolve sugar and gelatin; add lemon juice and rind. Blend well.
- Chill gelatin mixture until partially set. Beat until frothy. Add frothy gelatin mixture to the stiffly beaten egg whites. Continue to beat until the mixture begins to thicken.
- Turn mixture into a 4-cup (1 L) mold that has been rinsed with cold water. Chill until firm.
- To serve, unmold and decorate as desired.

VARIATIONS   *Apple Snow is made by adding 1 cup (250 mL) applesauce to sugar syrup, along with lemon juice and rind. Garnish or decorate with a light custard sauce or whipped cream. Add a dab of red currant or crab apple jelly to be really authentic.*

YIELD   ***5-6 SERVINGS***

PINEAPPLE DESSERT
THEY'LL ASK FOR SECONDS

2½ cups	graham wafer crumbs	625 mL
½ cup	melted butter	125 mL
1½ cups	icing sugar	375 mL
½ cup	softened butter	125 mL
2	eggs	2
14 oz.	can crushed pineapple, drained	398 mL
1 cup	whipping cream, whipped	250 mL

- Combine wafer crumbs and melted butter. Mix well. Reserve ½ cup (125 mL) of crumbs for topping. Press remaining crumb mixture into a lightly buttered 9 x 13" (23 x 32 cm) pan. Bake at 325°F (160°C) for 20 minutes. Cool.
- Combine icing sugar, softened butter and eggs. Beat well. Spread on top of cooled crumb base.
- Gently fold pineapple into whipped cream. Spread on top of icing sugar mixture.
- Sprinkle reserved crumbs on top.
- Refrigerate for 4 hours before serving.

YIELD   ***10-12 SERVINGS***

HINTS   *To whip cream, chill glass bowl and beaters well. To keep whipped cream firm, add 1 tbsp. (15 mL) of icing sugar rather than granulated sugar for every cup (250 mL) of whipping cream. Icing sugar contains cornstarch which helps to stabilize the whipped cream.*

LAYERED PUDDING DELIGHT

IF IT ISN'T YOUR FAVORITE YOU HAVEN'T TRIED IT!

BASE:

1 cup	flour	250 mL
½ cup	butter	125 mL
2 tbsp.	sugar	30 mL
¼ cup	chopped nuts	50 mL

FILLING:

8 oz.	cream cheese	250 g
⅔ cup	icing sugar	150 mL
1 cup	Cool Whip	250 mL

TOPPING:

2½ cups	milk	625 mL
2 x 3½ oz.	instant pudding mix	2 x 100 g
1 cup	Cool Whip	250 mL
	garnish *	

- To prepare the base, combine flour, butter, sugar and nuts. Mix until crumbly. Press into a greased 10" (25 cm) springform pan. Bake at 350°F (180°C) for 15 minutes. Cool.
- To prepare the filling, beat the cream cheese with the icing sugar. Add Cool Whip and continue to beat until well blended. Spread over cooled crust. Refrigerate while making topping.
- To prepare the topping, beat milk with pudding mix until thick. Pour over cheese layer. Top with remaining Cool Whip.
- * Garnish with coconut, chopped nuts, slivered almonds, shaved chocolate or as desired.

VARIATIONS	*Select your favorite pudding flavor, such as chocolate, butterscotch, lemon, pistachio or caramel. Select garnish to complement pudding flavor.*
	A chocolate wafer crumb crust is delicious with pistachio pudding.
YIELD	**12-16 SERVINGS**

APPLE CRISP
SO EASY AND SO GOOD!

6 cups	sliced apples	1.5 L
¼ cup	white sugar	50 mL
2 tbsp.	lemon juice	30 mL
¾ cup	rolled oats	175 mL
½ cup	brown sugar	125 mL
½ cup	flour	125 mL
1 tsp.	cinnamon	5 mL
⅓ cup	butter OR margarine	75 mL
	whipped cream OR ice cream for garnish	

- Arrange apples in a buttered 2-quart (2 L) ovenproof casserole. Sprinkle apples with white sugar and lemon juice.
- Combine rolled oats, sugar, flour and cinnamon. Cut in butter until mixture is crumbly and sprinkle over the apples.
- Bake at 350°F (180°C) for 40 minutes or until apples are tender.
- Serve warm with whipped cream or ice cream.

VARIATIONS   *Substitute chopped rhubarb, blueberries or saskatoons for the sliced apples.*

YIELD   *6 SERVINGS*

RHUBARB CRUMBLE

A TREAT FROM GRANDMA'S KITCHEN

1 cup	flour	250 mL
1 cup	brown sugar	250 mL
½ cup	melted butter	125 mL
¾ cup	oatmeal	175 mL
1 tsp.	cinnamon	5 mL
4 cups	chopped rhubarb	1 L
1 cup	white sugar	250 mL
2 tbsp.	cornstarch	30 mL
1 cup	water	250 mL
1 tsp.	vanilla	5 mL

- Mix flour, brown sugar, melted butter, oatmeal and cinnamon together until crumbly. Press half of the crumbs into the bottom and part way up the sides of a greased 9 x 13" (23 x 32 cm) pan. Set remaining crumbs aside.
- Sprinkle rhubarb over oatmeal base.
- In a saucepan, combine sugar, cornstarch, water and vanilla. Heat to boiling. Cook and stir until thickened. Pour over rhubarb.
- Place remaining crumbs on top.
- Bake at 350°F (180°C) for 45-60 minutes. Serve warm.

VARIATIONS   *Chopped apples and/or blueberries, peaches or pears may replace some or all of the rhubarb depending on availability and desired flavor.*

YIELD   **8 SERVINGS**

RICE PUDDING

THE ULTIMATE IN COMFORT FOOD!

3 cups	milk	750 mL
¼ cup	long-grain rice	50 mL
¼ cup	sugar	50 mL
¼ tsp.	salt	1 mL
½ tsp.	vanilla	2 mL
¼ tsp.	nutmeg	1 mL
¼ tsp.	cinnamon	1 mL
½ cup	raisins	125 mL

- Mix all ingredients together.
- Pour mixture into a buttered 6-cup (1.5 L) ovenproof casserole.
- Bake at 350°F (180°C) for 2 hours or until rice is tender. While pudding is baking, stir occasionally to mix the surface skin, which forms, into the pudding.
- Serve warm or cold. Drizzle with maple syrup, if you wish.

YIELD   6 SERVINGS

BREAD PUDDING

THIS WILL BRING BACK CHILDHOOD MEMORIES.

2 cups	milk	500 mL
4 cups	cubed stale bread	1 L
1 cup	brown sugar	250 mL
⅓ cup	melted butter	75 mL
2	eggs	2
2 tsp.	vanilla	10 mL
1 cup	raisins	250 mL
1 cup	coconut (optional)	250 mL

- In a mixing bowl, add milk to bread.
- In a separate bowl, combine the remaining ingredients; beat well and add to the bread mixture.
- Pour into a buttered 6-cup (1.6 L) ovenproof casserole.
- Bake at 350°F (180°C) for 1 hour.
- If desired, serve with a sauce. Try the Lemon Sauce, page 122, or Caramel Sauce, page 135.

YIELD   8 SERVINGS

APPLE PUDDING

A WONDERFUL WINTERTIME DESSERT

½ cup	shortening	125 mL
2 cups	sugar	500 mL
2	eggs	2
2 cups	flour	500 mL
2 tsp.	baking soda	10 mL
1 tsp.	salt	5 mL
1 tsp.	nutmeg	5 mL
1 tsp.	cinnamon	5 mL
1 cup	chopped nuts	250 mL
6	apples, finely chopped	6

- Cream shortening and sugar. Add eggs and beat well.
- Sift dry ingredients together. Add to creamed mixture. Blend thoroughly. Batter will be stiff at this point.
- Stir in nuts and apples.
- Turn batter into a greased 9 x 13" (23 x 32 cm) pan.
- Bake at 350°F (180°C) for 40-50 minutes.
- Serve warm with Lemon Sauce, below.

LEMON SAUCE

1 cup	sugar	250 mL
1 tbsp.	cornstarch	15 mL
1 tbsp.	butter	15 mL
1 cup	boiling water	250 mL
¼ cup	lemon juice	50 mL

- Combine all ingredients in a saucepan, boil for 5 minutes. Serve over Apple Pudding.

YIELD: ***10 SERVINGS***

SAUCED PUDDING

MAKES ITS OWN CARAMEL SAUCE

1 cup	flour	250 mL
2 tsp.	baking powder	10 mL
2 tsp.	sugar	10 mL
¼ tsp.	salt	1 mL
2 tbsp.	shortening	30 mL
1 cup	raisins	250 mL
½ cup	milk	125 mL
1 tsp.	vanilla	5 mL
1 cup	brown sugar	250 mL
2 tbsp.	butter	30 mL
1¾ cups	boiling water	425 mL

- Grease a 6-cup (1.5 L) overproof casserole.
- In a mixing bowl, blend together the flour, baking powder, sugar and salt.
- With a pastry blender, cut the shortening into the dry ingredients until the mixture resembles coarse meal.
- Stir in raisins.
- Combine the milk and vanilla and stir into mixture with a fork. Batter will be quite stiff.
- Pour the batter into the prepared casserole.
- Mix together brown sugar, butter and boiling water. Pour over batter in casserole.
- Bake at 375°F (190°C) for 30 minutes or until golden brown. As the pudding bakes the batter will rise and a caramel sauce will form in the bottom of the dish.

YIELD: *6 SERVINGS*

CREAM PUFFS

THESE ARE NOT DIFFICULT AND THEY LOOK AND TASTE WONDERFUL

1 cup	water	250 mL
½ cup	butter OR margarine	125 mL
1 cup	flour	250 mL
¼ tsp.	salt	1 mL
4	eggs	4

- In a saucepan, heat water and butter until water boils and butter melts. Then lower heat.
- Combine flour and salt. Add to saucepan. Beat vigorously until mixture leaves the side of the pan.
- Remove from heat. Add eggs, 1 at a time, beating well after each addition.
- Drop mixture on lightly greased cookie sheet to form 10 puffs.
- Bake at 400°F (200°C) for 50 minutes. Cool on rack.
- When cool, cut tops, scoop out center, soft dough.
- Fill with whipped cream, fruit or custard. Drizzle a chocolate or fruit sauce on top. Serve.

VARIATIONS   *To make Éclairs, with a pastry tube, pipe cream puff paste onto cookie sheets, in 4" (10 cm) lengths. Bake as above. Fill with whipped cream or chocolate or coffee-flavored custard. Chocolate frosting or sauce adds a luxurious finish.*

YIELD   ***10 PUFFS***

APPLE PIE

A FOREVER FAVORITE!

	pastry for 2-crust pie, page 133	
4 cups	pared, sliced apples	1 L
½ cup	brown sugar	125 mL
½ cup	white sugar	125 mL
2 tbsp.	flour	30 mL
½ tsp.	nutmeg	2 mL
1 tsp.	cinnamon	5 mL
1 tbsp.	butter	15 mL

- Line a 9" (23 cm) pie plate with pastry.
- Combine apples with sugar, flour and spices. Turn into pie plate and dot with butter.
- Cover filling with top crust. Seal and flute edges of pastry. Prick top crust with a fork.
- Bake at 425°F (220°C) for 10 minutes. Reduce heat to 350°F (180°C), continue to bake for an additional 55 minutes or until crust is golden brown.

YIELD   *6 SERVINGS*

HINTS   *To make a golden brown pie crust, brush top crust with milk and sprinkle with sugar before baking.*

APPLE RAISIN PECAN PIE

RAISINS SOAKED IN PEACH SCHNAPPS MAKE THIS PIE UNIQUE!

½ cup	raisins	125 mL
2 tbsp.	peach schnapps	30 mL
¼ cup	softened butter	50 mL
1 cup	pecan halves	250 mL
⅔ cup	brown sugar	150 mL
6-8	apples, sliced	6-8
	pastry for a 2-crust pie, page 133	
2 tbsp.	lemon juice	30 mL
1 tbsp.	flour	15 mL
½ cup	white sugar	125 mL
1 tsp.	cinnamon	5 mL
½ tsp.	nutmeg	2 mL
¼ tsp.	salt	1 mL
1 tsp.	grated lemon peel (optional)	5 mL
½ cup	whipping cream, whipped (optional)	125 mL

- Soak raisins in peach schnapps for several hours. Drain well.
- In a 10" (25 cm) pie plate spread butter evenly over the bottom and sides. Press pecans, round side down, into the butter. Sprinkle brown sugar over the nuts.
- Roll out pastry. Line pie plate with pastry, over the pecan layer.
- Combine raisins, apples and the remaining ingredients, except whipped cream. Mix well. Pour into pie crust. Place top pastry over filling mixture. Crimp pastry edges. Prick top crust with a fork.
- Bake at 450°F (230°C) for 10 minutes. Reduce heat to 350°F (180°C) and continue to bake for 40 minutes or until golden brown.
- Cool pie on a rack until filling stops bubbling. Place serving plate over pie. Carefully invert. Remove pie plate.
- If desired, garnish with whipped cream to serve.

YIELD   **10 SERVINGS**

See photograph opposite page 128.

RAISIN PIE

ALWAYS POPULAR AT PICNICS AND FOWL SUPPERS

2 cups	seedless raisins	500 mL
2 cups	water	500 mL
½ cup	sugar	125 mL
2 tbsp.	flour	30 mL
⅛ tsp.	salt	0.5 mL
½ tsp.	vanilla	2 mL
1 tbsp.	butter	15 mL
1 tbsp.	lemon juice	15 mL
	pastry for a 2-crust 9" pie, page 133	

- In a saucepan, combine raisins and water. Simmer for 10 minutes.
- Combine sugar, flour and salt. Gradually stir into raisin mixture over heat. Cook until mixture has thickened. Remove from heat.
- Blend in vanilla, butter and lemon juice. Cool.
- Line a 9" (23 cm) pie plate with pastry. Pour raisin mixture into pie plate. Cover with top crust. Seal and flute edges of pastry. Prick top crust with a fork.
- Bake at 450°F (230°C) for 15 minutes. Reduce heat to 350°F (180°C) and bake for an additional 40 minutes.

YIELD   *6-8 SERVINGS*

RHUBARB AND STRAWBERRY PIE
ONE OF THE BEST PIES OF THE SUMMER SEASON!

	pastry for a 2-crust pie, page 133	
1 cup	sliced strawberries	250 mL
4 cups	chopped rhubarb	1 L
1¼ cups	sugar	300 mL
¼ cup	cornstarch (or minute tapioca)	50 mL
½ tsp.	cinnamon	2 mL
1 tbsp.	milk	15 mL
	sugar	

- Line the bottom of a 9" (23 cm) pie plate with pie crust.
- Combine all ingredients except milk and sugar.
- Pour into pie crust. Top with a lattice-type crust. Brush with milk and sprinkle with sugar.
- Bake at 350°F (180°C) for 1 hour or until golden brown.

VARIATIONS   *Blueberries or saskatoons may be substituted for the strawberries.*

YIELD   ***6 SERVINGS***

HINTS   *A lattice top crust prevents the pie juices from running over.*

Apple Raisin Pecan Pie, page 126
Peach Schnapps

CRUMB-TOPPED PIES

ENJOY THE BEST OF EACH FRUIT IN SEASON.

pastry for a 1-crust pie, page 133

FILLING:

4 cups	berries OR chopped fruit	1 L
½-¾ cup	sugar	125-175 mL
¼ cup	cornstarch OR minute tapioca	50 mL
1 tsp.	cinnamon (optional)	5 mL
½ tsp.	nutmeg (optional)	2 mL
1 tbsp.	lemon juice (optional)	15 mL

CRUMB TOPPING:

⅓ cup	brown sugar	75 mL
¼ cup	flour	50 mL
¼ cup	butter	50 mL
1 tsp.	cinnamon (optional)	5 mL

- Line a 9" (23 cm) pie plate with pastry.
- Combine berries or fruit with sugar, cornstarch, spices and lemon juice. Mix gently but thoroughly. Pour filling into pie crust.
- Combine ingredients for topping until crumbly. Sprinkle crumbs over filling.
- Bake at 350°F (180°C) for 1 hour.

VARIATIONS   *Suggested fruits to use are apples, peaches, apricots, plums, pears, blueberries, saskatoons and raspberries.*
The amount of sugar and the type of spices used will vary with the type of fruit and the sweetness desired.

YIELD   ***6 SERVINGS***

See photograph on front cover.

HINTS   *Rhubarb added to saskatoons softens the berries.*

PUMPKIN PIE

A THANKSGIVING FAVORITE FOR WHICH YOU WILL BE TRULY THANKFUL!

1 cup	sugar	250 mL
1 tbsp.	flour	15 mL
½ tsp.	salt	2 mL
2 tsp.	pumpkin pie spice *	10 mL
3	large eggs	3
1½ cups	mashed pumpkin	375 mL
1 cup	light cream	250 mL
	9" (23 cm) unbaked pie shell, page 133	
	whipped cream for garnish (optional)	

- Mix the sugar, flour, salt and spices together. Beat in the eggs. Stir in the pumpkin and cream.
- Pour mixture into pie shell.
- Bake at 400°F (200°C) for 10 minutes. Reduce heat to 350°F (180°C) and bake 45 minutes or until the tip of a knife, inserted in the center of the pie, comes out clean.
- If desired, garnish with whipped cream.

* Or, make your own by combining 1 tsp. (5 mL) cinnamon, ½ tsp. (2 mL) ginger, ¼ tsp. (1 mL) each nutmeg, allspice and cloves.

YIELD   *6 SERVINGS*

LEMON MERINGUE PIE

BEAUTIFUL TO LOOK AT — A TREAT TO EAT!

	9" (23 cm) baked pie shell, page 133	
⅓ cup	cornstarch	75 mL
1 cup	sugar	250 mL
2 cups	cold water	500 mL
3	egg yolks	3
¼ cup	butter	50 mL
⅓ cup	lemon juice	75 mL
1½ tsp.	grated lemon rind	7 mL
1½ tsp.	lemon extract	7 mL

- Prepare pie shell.
- In a double boiler, combine cornstarch and sugar. Gradually add water, mixing well. Cook, stirring constantly, until mixture thickens and is clear.
- Beat egg yolks until lemon colored. Stir a small amount of cornstarch mixture into egg yolks. Return to cornstarch mixture. Cook, stirring constantly, for 2 more minutes.
- Remove from heat. Add butter, lemon juice, rind and extract. Mix well and cool.
- Pour cooled lemon filing into pie shell. Cool.

YIELD   *6 SERVINGS*

MERINGUE:

3	egg whites	3
⅓ cup	sugar	75 mL
½ tsp.	cream of tartar	2 mL

- Beat egg whites until fluffy. While continuing to beat, gradually add sugar and cream of tartar. Beat until stiff peaks form.
- Spread meringue over cooled pie filling. Seal all edges so that meringue does not shrink during baking.
- Bake pie at 350°F (180°C) for 10 minutes or until meringue is golden brown.

HINTS   *Before cutting a pie with a meringue, dip the knife in boiling water to prevent the meringue from crumbling or tearing.*

FLAPPER PIE

A SUNDAY DINNER SPECIAL!

1½ cups	graham wafer crumbs	375 mL
½ cup	sugar	125 mL
½ tsp.	cinnamon	2 mL
½ cup	melted butter	125 mL
2 tbsp.	cornstarch	30 mL
½ cup	sugar	125 mL
2 cups	milk	500 mL
½ tsp.	vanilla	2 mL
3	egg yolks	3
3	egg whites	3
½ cup	sugar	125 mL

- Combine crumbs, sugar and cinnamon. Add melted butter and mix well. Reserve ½ cup (125 mL) of crumbs for topping. Press the remainder of the crumbs into the bottom and sides of a 9" (23 cm) pie plate. Bake at 350°F (180°C) for 15 minutes.
- Combine cornstarch, sugar and ½ cup (125 mL) of the milk. Mix well.
- In a double boiler, bring the other 1½ cups (375 mL) of milk to a boil. Add the cornstarch mixture. Cook for 5 minutes.
- Combine vanilla with egg yolks. Add a bit of the hot cornstarch mixture to the yolks. Mix well. Return to the cornstarch mixture. Cook for 1 more minute. Pour into pie crust.
- Beat egg whites until frothy. Gradually add ½ cup (125 mL) sugar while continuing to beat until stiff peaks form. Spread meringue over filling. Seal all edges. Sprinkle with reserved crumbs.
- Bake at 325°F (160°C) for 25 minutes.
- Cool for a few hours before serving.

YIELD   *6 SERVINGS*

PIE PASTRY

5 cups	flour	1.25 L
1 tsp.	salt	5 mL
1 tsp.	baking powder	5 mL
1 tbsp.	brown sugar	15 mL
1 lb.	lard	500 g
⅔ cup	cold water	150 mL
1	egg	1
2 tbsp.	vinegar	30 mL

- Mix together flour, salt, baking powder, and sugar.
- With a pastry blender, cut in the lard.
- Beat together the water, egg, and vinegar. Stir into the lard mixture
- Chill pastry to make it easier to handle.
- Bring pastry to room temperature before rolling out. For a 2-crust pie, divide dough into 2, evenly, before rolling it.
- Lightly flour the rolling surface and the rolling pin.
- Roll dough, from the center out, to an ⅛" (3 mm) thickness or less. Patch any tears, do not reroll dough! Roll dough about 2" (5 cm) larger than pie plate dimensions. Save trimmings to make decorative appliques (apples, berries, hearts, holly, etc.) for top crust.
- This freezes well.

YIELD   *PASTRY FOR APPROXIMATELY 6, 8" (20 CM) DOUBLE-CRUST PIES.*

APPLE CAKE

A WARM INVITING AUTUMN FAVORITE

2 cups	flour	500 mL
4 tsp.	baking powder	20 mL
¼ tsp.	salt	1 mL
4 tbsp.	butter	60 mL
⅔ cup	milk	150 mL
5	apples, pared, sliced	5
3 tbsp.	butter	45 mL
1 tsp.	cinnamon	5 mL
1 cup	brown sugar	250 mL

- Combine flour, baking powder, salt and butter. Stir in milk. Press into a greased 9" (23 cm) pan.
- Place apple slices on top of base.
- Combine the butter, cinnamon and brown sugar. Sprinkle over apple slices.
- Bake at 375°F (190°C) for 20-25 minutes or until apples are tender.

SERVING *Serve warm with ice cream or whipping cream.*
SUGGESTION

YIELD **12 SERVINGS**

APPLE CAKE WITH CARAMEL SAUCE

A RICH MOIST CAKE WITH A BUTTERY CARAMEL TOPPING

3	eggs, beaten	3
2 cups	sugar	500 mL
2 tsp.	vanilla	10 mL
1½ cups	cooking oil	375 mL
3 cups	flour	750 mL
1 tsp.	baking soda	5 mL
2 tsp.	cinnamon	10 mL
½ tsp.	salt	2 mL
4	apples, peeled, cored, chopped	4
1 cup	chopped walnuts	250 mL

- In a mixing bowl, combine eggs, sugar, vanilla and oil. Set aside.
- In another bowl, combine the flour, baking soda, cinnamon and salt.
- Add the apples and walnuts to the dry ingredients.
- Fold the liquid ingredients into the dry mixture.
- Pour batter into a greased bundt pan.
- Bake at 325°F (160°C) for 1½ hours or until inserted toothpick comes out clean.
- Cool on cake rack for 15 minutes before removing from pan.
- Serve as is or with Caramel Sauce, recipe follows.

CARAMEL SAUCE

½ cup	white sugar	125 mL
½ cup	brown sugar	125 mL
½ cup	butter	125 mL
½ cup	whipping cream	125 mL

- Combine all ingredients in a small saucepan. Bring to a boil. Cook 1 minute. Serve with Apple Cake.

YIELD   *16 SERVINGS*

PINEAPPLE UPSIDE-DOWN CAKE

AN OLD-TIME SPECIALTY — TRY VARIATIONS WITH YOUR FAVORITE FRUIT

¼ cup	butter	50 mL
1 cup	brown sugar	250 mL
5-6	whole pineapple slices	5-6
6	maraschino cherries	6
12	pecan halves (optional)	12
½ cup	butter	125 mL
1 cup	sugar	250 mL
2	eggs	2
2 cups	flour	500 mL
2 tsp.	baking powder	10 mL
¼ tsp.	salt	1 mL
¾ cup	milk	175 mL

- In a 10" (25 cm) round baking dish, melt butter, then add brown sugar. Stir until smooth and evenly distributed in pan.
- Arrange pineapple slices in brown sugar mixture. Place a cherry in the center of each pineapple slice. Arrange pecan halves between slices.
- Cream ½ cup (125 mL) butter with sugar. Add eggs and beat well.
- Combine flour, baking powder and salt. Add dry ingredients alternately with milk to creamed mixture. Pour gently over arranged fruit.
- Bake at 350°F (180°C) for 50 minutes or until an inserted toothpick comes out clean.
- Remove from oven and turn out (upside down) on a serving plate, immediately.
- Cool before serving.

VARIATIONS *The cake batter may be exchanged for a small white or yellow cake mix prepared according to package directions.*

Various fruits may be substituted for the pineapple and cherries, try peaches, apricots or apples.

YIELD **8 SERVINGS**

WHITE CAKE

THIS BASIC CAKE MAY BE USED FOR SHORTCAKE, TRIFLE OR
JUST ICED AND TOPPED WITH COCONUT

1 cup	sugar	250 mL
½ cup	butter	125 mL
2	eggs	2
2 cups	flour	500 mL
¼ tsp.	salt	1 mL
2 tsp.	baking powder	10 mL
1 cup	milk	250 mL
1 tsp.	vanilla extract	5 mL
½ tsp.	almond extract	2 mL

- In a mixing bowl, beat sugar, butter and eggs together.
- In another bowl, combine flour, salt and baking powder.
- Combine the milk and the flavorings. Add milk alternately with the dry ingredients to the creamed mixture.
- Pour batter into 2 greased and floured 8" (20 cm) round pans.
- Bake at 350°F (180°C) for 25 minutes or until cake springs back when lightly touched.

YIELD   **16 SERVINGS**

POPPY SEED LEMON CAKE
A LIGHT CAKE WITH A RICH LEMON FILLING

3 cups	flour	750 mL
4 tsp.	baking powder	20 mL
1 tsp.	salt	5 mL
2 cups	unsalted butter	500 mL
2 cups	sugar	500 mL
2 tsp.	vanilla	10 mL
6	eggs, at room temperature	6
⅔ cup	milk	150 mL
½ cup	poppy seeds	125 mL

- Combine the flour, baking powder and salt.
- In another bowl, beat the butter until creamy. Gradually add the sugar and vanilla and continue to beat until light and fluffy.
- Add eggs, 1 at a time, to the creamed mixture. Beat well after each addition.
- Add milk alternately with the dry ingredients, beginning and ending with the dry ingredients. Be careful not to overbeat.
- Fold poppy seeds gently into the batter.
- Turn batter into 2 well-greased and floured 9" (23 cm) round, 2" (5 cm) deep cake pans.
- Bake at 350°F (180°C) for 45-50 minutes or until cake springs back when lightly touched.
- Cool on racks for 5 minutes before removing cake from pans. Cool completely.
- To assemble cake, horizontally slice each layer in half to form 4 layers. Spread Lemon Butter (recipe follows) between layers. Frost with Cream Cheese Frosting, page 149 or, for lemon lovers, try a Lemon Butter Frosting. Decorate with lemon zest. Refrigerate until ready to serve.

YIELD   *16 SERVINGS*

See photograph opposite page 144.

HINTS   *To split a cake into layers insert toothpicks into the side as markers. "Saw" through with a length of nylon thread.*

LEMON BUTTER

2	eggs	2
6 tbsp.	lemon juice	90 mL
2 tbsp.	grated lemon rind	30 mL
1 cup	sugar	250 mL
¼ cup	butter	50 mL

- In a heavy saucepan, beat eggs with a fork until well blended.
- Stir in lemon juice, lemon rind and sugar. Add butter.
- Cook over low heat until thickened.
- Cool. Store in refrigerator.

**SERVING
SUGGESTIONS**
Spoon Lemon Butter into baked tart shells. Use as filling between cake layers.

YIELD
APPROXIMATELY 1¼ CUPS (300 mL)

RED VELVET CAKE

A MOIST, INTERESTING CAKE FOR THAT SPECIAL OCCASION!

¾ cup	oil	175 mL
1 cup	sugar	250 mL
2	eggs	2
2 tbsp.	red food coloring	30 mL
2 cups	flour	500 mL
1 tsp.	baking powder	5 mL
¼ tsp.	salt	1 mL
1 tsp.	cocoa	5 mL
1 tsp.	baking soda	5 mL
1 tsp.	vinegar	5 mL
1 cup	buttermilk	250 mL
1 tsp.	vanilla	5 mL
¾ cup	milk	175 mL
½ cup	sugar	125 mL

- In a mixing bowl, beat together oil and sugar. Add eggs, 1 at a time, beating well after each addition. Add food coloring, mix well.
- Sift together flour, baking powder, salt and cocoa.
- In a separate bowl, dissolve baking soda in vinegar. Stir vinegar mixture into buttermilk; add vanilla.
- Add dry ingredients, alternately with buttermilk mixture, to egg mixture. Beat until smooth.
- Pour batter into 2 well-greased and floured 9" (23 cm) round pans.
- Bake at 350°F (180°C) for 25 minutes or until an inserted toothpick comes out clean.
- While cake is baking, in a saucepan, combine milk and sugar. Bring to a boil, then cool. When cake layers are baked, set out on racks and let cool for 5 minutes. Put waxed paper under racks. Prick holes in layers. Pour milk-sugar mixture over and allow to soak into layers.
- Put layers together and frost with frosting of your choice or use Coconut-Cream Cheese Frosting which follows.

YIELD   *16 SERVINGS*

COCONUT-CREAM CHEESE FROSTING

8 oz.	cream cheese	250 g
½ cup	butter	125 mL
1 tsp.	vanilla	5 mL
1 cup	icing sugar	250 mL
¾ cup	flaked coconut	175 mL
4	drops red food coloring	4
¼ cup	flaked coconut	50 mL

- Beat together the cheese, butter and vanilla. Beat in the sugar and coconut.
- Combine remaining coconut with food coloring. Sprinkle on top of cake.

YIELD   *MAKES ENOUGH TO FROST A 2-LAYER CAKE*

MEXICAN WEDDING CAKE

2	eggs	2
2 cups	sugar	500 mL
2 tsp.	baking soda	10 mL
14 oz.	can crushed pineapple, undrained	398 mL
2 cups	flour	500 mL
2 tsp.	vanilla	10 mL
1 cup	chopped walnuts	250 mL
1 cup	shredded sweetened coconut (optional)	250 mL

- Combine all ingredients and mix well.
- Pour into a greased 9 x 13" (23 x 32 cm) pan.
- Bake at 350°F (180°C) for 45 minutes or until cake springs back when lightly touched.
- Frost with Cream Cheese Frosting, page 149, while cake is warm.

YIELD   *24 SERVINGS*

LAZY DAISY CAKE

ADULTS & KIDS WILL EQUALLY ENJOY THIS SELF-ICED TREAT!

2	eggs	2
1 cup	sugar	250 mL
1 tsp.	vanilla	5 mL
1 cup	flour	250 mL
1 tsp.	baking powder	5 mL
¼ tsp.	salt	1 mL
½ cup	milk	125 mL
1 tbsp.	butter	15 mL

TOPPING

1 cup	chopped nuts OR grated coconut	250 mL
½ cup	brown sugar	125 mL
½ cup	melted butter	125 mL
¼ cup	cream	50 mL
1 tsp.	vanilla	5 mL

- Beat eggs in a large bowl, gradually add sugar to eggs. Continue beating until thick and light. Add vanilla.
- In a separate bowl, combine flour, baking powder and salt. Stir into the egg mixture.
- Bring milk to the boiling point. Add butter to milk. Stir into the egg mixture. Beat well.
- Pour into a greased and floured 9" (23 cm) square pan.
- Bake at 350°F (180°C) for 30 minutes.
- To prepare topping, combine all ingredients.
- When cake is baked but still hot, spread with topping mixture. Place cake under the broiler until the topping is bubbly and brown (about 4-5 minutes when placed about 6" [15 cm] from the broiler). Watch carefully!

YIELD   *16 SERVINGS*

CHOCOLATE CAKE
A PERENNIAL FAVORITE!

1 cup	brown sugar	250 mL
½ cup	butter	125 mL
1 tbsp.	corn syrup	15 mL
2	eggs	2
1½ cups	flour	375 mL
2 tsp.	baking powder	10 mL
1 tsp.	baking soda	5 mL
3 tbsp.	cocoa	45 mL
⅛ tsp.	salt	0.5 mL
1 cup	cold water	250 mL
1 tsp.	vanilla	5 mL

- Cream together, sugar, butter, syrup and eggs.
- In a separate bowl, combine flour, baking powder, baking soda, cocoa and salt.
- Add dry ingredients, alternately with cold water, to the creamed mixture. Stir in vanilla. Beat well.
- Pour batter into a greased 9" (23 cm) square pan.
- Bake at 350°F (180°C) for 30 minutes or until an inserted toothpick comes out clean. Frost cake, when cool with Easy Fudge Icing, page 149, OR Chocolate Butter Icing, page 158.

YIELD   *16 SERVINGS*

CHOCOLATE SPICE CAKE

CLOVES AND CINNAMON HEIGHTEN THE CHOCOLATE FLAVOR

½ cup	shortening	125 mL
¾ cup	sugar	175 mL
1	egg	1
½ cup	sugar	125 mL
¼ cup	cocoa	50 mL
½ tsp.	ground cloves	2 mL
½ tsp.	cinnamon	2 mL
1½ cups	flour	375 mL
1 tsp.	baking soda	5 mL
½ tsp.	salt	2 mL
1 cup	buttermilk	250 mL
½ tsp.	vanilla	2 mL

- In a mixing bowl, beat shortening with ¾ cup (175 mL) sugar. Add egg, beat well.
- Mix ½ cup (125 mL) sugar with cocoa, cloves and cinnamon. Stir into creamed mixture.
- Combine flour, baking soda and salt. Add alternately with buttermilk. Mix well, then add vanilla.
- Pour batter into a greased and floured 9" (23 cm) square pan.
- Bake at 375°F (190°C) for 30 minutes or until center of cake springs back when lightly touched. Cool and frost, if desired, or sprinkle with icing sugar.

YIELD   *16 SERVINGS*

HINTS   *To retain their flavor and color, spices should be stored in a cool dry place, not near the kitchen stove.*

Poppy Seed Lemon Cake, page 138
Lemon Butter, page 139

ZUCCHINI CHOCOLATE CAKE

A VERY MOIST LUSCIOUS CAKE

½ cup	vegetable oil	125 mL
1½ cups	sugar	375 mL
2	eggs	2
1 tsp.	vanilla	5 mL
2 cups	grated, unpeeled zucchini	500 mL
2 cups	flour	500 mL
¼ cup	cocoa	50 mL
½ tsp.	baking powder	2 mL
1 tsp.	baking soda	5 mL
½ tsp.	cinnamon	2 mL
½ tsp.	ground cloves	2 mL
¾ cup	sour cream	175 mL
½ cup	chocolate chips	125 mL

- In a large mixing bowl, beat oil and sugar together. Add eggs and mix well. Stir in vanilla and zucchini.
- In another bowl, combine flour, cocoa, baking powder, baking soda, cinnamon and cloves. Add to creamed mixture alternately with sour cream. Mix well.
- Stir in chocolate chips.
- Pour batter into a greased 9 x 13" (23 x 32 cm) baking pan.
- Bake at 325°F (160°C) oven for 45 minutes or until center springs back when pressed lightly with fingertip.
- Cool, then frost with Chocolate Butter Icing, page 158. If desired sprinkle with additional chocolate chips.

VARIATIONS   *For a more deluxe presentation, bake this cake in a bundt pan and drizzle cooled cake with thinned Chocolate Icing or Chocolate Sauce.*

YIELD   ***16 SERVINGS***

BOILED RAISIN CAKE

THIS CAKE, POPULAR DURING THE WAR YEARS, WAS AN EGGLESS, BUTTERLESS, MILKLESS WONDER.
THIS MODERN VERSION USES BUTTER TO REPLACE THE LARD USED IN EARLIER RECIPES.

1 cup	brown sugar	250 mL
½ cup	butter	125 mL
1 cup	cold water	250 mL
1½ cups	raisins	375 mL
1 tsp.	cinnamon	5 mL
1 tsp.	nutmeg	5 mL
½ tsp.	ground cloves	2 mL
2 cups	flour	500 mL
1½ tsp.	baking soda	7 mL

- In a saucepan, combine sugar, butter, water, raisins and spices. Bring to a boil and continue to boil for 3 minutes. Then cool.
- In a separate bowl, combine flour and baking soda. Stir into the cooled raisin mixture.
- Pour into a greased and floured 9" (23 cm) square pan.
- Bake at 350°F (180°C) for 25 minutes or until cake springs back when touched lightly.
- Sprinkle lightly with icing sugar.

YIELD   **12 SERVINGS**

HINTS   *Raisins stored in a jar with about ¼ cup (50 mL) of dry sherry or rum, will stay plump and flavorful for use in puddings, cakes and muffins.*

CARROT CAKE

THERE ARE CARROT CAKES AND THEN THERE IS THIS SIMPLE BUT DELICIOUS CARROT CAKE!

½ cup	oil	125 mL
1 cup	brown sugar	250 mL
2	eggs	2
1½ cups	flour	375 mL
1 tsp.	baking soda	5 mL
1 tsp.	baking powder	5 mL
⅛ tsp.	salt	0.5 mL
1 tsp.	cinnamon	5 mL
½ cup	milk	125 mL
1 cup	grated carrots	250 mL

- In a mixing bowl, combine oil, sugar and eggs. Beat well.
- In another bowl, combine flour, baking soda, baking powder, salt and cinnamon.
- Add dry ingredients, alternately with the milk, to the egg mixture.
- Stir in grated carrots.
- Pour into a greased 9" (23 cm) square baking pan.
- Bake at 350°F (180°C) for 30 minutes or until cake springs back when lightly touched near the center.
- Ice with Cream Cheese Frosting, page 149.

VARIATIONS *Substitute an equivalent amount of grated zucchini for grated carrots.*

YIELD *16 SERVINGS*

PUMPKIN ROLL

JELLY-ROLL EXTRAORDINAIRE!

3	eggs, beaten	3
1 cup	sugar	250 mL
⅔ cup	cooked pumpkin	150 mL
1 tsp.	lemon juice	5 mL
¾ cup	flour	175 mL
2 tsp.	cinnamon	10 mL
1 tsp.	baking powder	5 mL
1 tsp.	ground ginger	5 mL
½ tsp.	salt	2 mL
½ tsp.	nutmeg	2 mL
1 cup	chopped walnuts	250 mL
	Cream Cheese Frosting, page 149	

- In mixing bowl, beat eggs and sugar. Add the pumpkin and juice. Blend well.
- In another bowl, stir together, the flour, cinnamon, baking powder, ginger, salt and nutmeg. Add to the creamed mixture and beat until just blended. Do not overmix.
- Spread batter in a greased and floured 10 x 15" (25 x 38 cm) baking or jelly roll pan.
- Sprinkle nuts over batter.
- Bake at 375°F (190°C) for 15 minutes.
- Turn out onto a tea towel sprinkled with icing sugar. While still warm, roll up cake and towel together starting at the long side and keeping the nuts on the outside of the roll. Cool.
- Prepare Cream Cheese Frosting.
- Unroll cooled cake. Spread with frosting.
- Re-roll cake without tea towel. Chill for at least 4 hours.
- Slice to serve.

If tightly wrapped, this freezes well.

YIELD   *12 SERVINGS*

CREAM CHEESE FROSTING

4 oz.	cream cheese	125 g
¼ cup	butter OR margarine	50 mL
1 tsp.	vanilla	5 mL
2-2½ cups	icing sugar	500-625 mL

- Beat cream cheese, butter and vanilla until smooth. Add icing sugar to obtain desired spreading consistency.
- Use as a filling or frosting for your favorite cake recipes.

YIELD   *APPROXIMATELY 2 CUPS (500 mL) OF FROSTING. ANY EXTRA MAY BE FROZEN FOR FUTURE USE.*

FLUFFY CREAMY ICING

A MOCK WHIPPED CREAM ICING!

⅔ cup	icing sugar	150 mL
3 tbsp.	butter	45 mL
2 tbsp.	half and half cream	30 mL
1 tsp.	vanilla	5 mL
1 tsp.	boiling water	5 mL

- In a mixing bowl, combine all ingredients. Whip for 10 minutes.

NOTE   *It is essential to use half and half cream. DO NOT SUBSTITUTE with milk.*

YIELD   *ICING FOR A SINGLE LAYER CAKE*

EASY FUDGE ICING

½ cup	butter	125 mL
1 cup	brown sugar	250 mL
¼ cup	milk	50 mL
1¾-2 cups	icing sugar	425-500 mL

- In a saucepan, melt butter; stir in sugar and bring to a boil. Boil for 2 minutes while stirring constantly.
- Stir in milk and return to a boil. Cool to lukewarm.
- Gradually stir in icing sugar to obtain desired spreading consistency.

YIELD   *ENOUGH ICING FOR A 2-LAYER CAKE*

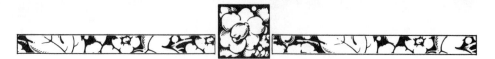

GINGERSNAP COOKIES

THESE HAVE AN OLD-FASHIONED "SNAP" TO THEM

¾ cup	butter	175 mL
1 cup	sugar	250 mL
¼ cup	molasses	50 mL
1	egg	1
2 cups	flour	500 mL
2 tsp.	baking soda	10 mL
1 tsp.	ginger	5 mL
1 tsp.	cinnamon	5 mL
1 tsp.	cloves	5 mL
	sugar	

- In a mixing bowl, beat butter, sugar, molasses and egg until light and fluffy.
- Combine flour, baking soda, ginger, cinnamon and cloves. Stir into the creamed mixture. Place dough in refrigerator for 2-4 hours.
- Shape dough into 1" (2.5 cm) balls and roll in sugar. Place balls about 3" (7 cm) apart on lightly greased cookie sheets. Do not flatten balls.
- Bake at 350°F (180°C) for 10-12 minutes.

YIELD   ***ABOUT 5 DOZEN COOKIES. THIS RECIPE DOUBLES WELL***

HINTS   *Shape 10-12 balls, place in a paper bag with sugar and shake gently.*

PEANUT BUTTER COOKIES

CRUMBLY, RICH AND FILLED WITH MEMORIES

1 cup	soft butter	250 mL
1 cup	peanut butter	250 mL
½ cup	white sugar	125 mL
½ cup	brown sugar	125 mL
2	eggs	2
2½ cups	flour	625 mL
1 tsp.	baking powder	5 mL
1½ tsp.	baking soda	7 mL
½ tsp.	salt	2 mL

- In a large mixing bowl, beat butter, peanut butter, sugars and eggs until light and fluffy.
- In a separate bowl, combine the dry ingredients. Add to the creamed mixture and blend well.
- Shape dough into balls and place on a lightly greased cookie sheet. Press balls down with a fork dipped in flour.
- Bake at 350°F (180°C) for 10-12 minutes or until lightly browned.

YIELD   **APPROXIMATELY 6 DOZEN**

OATMEAL CHOCOLATE CHIP COOKIES

A KID'S FAVORITE FOR LUNCHES OR PARTIES

1 cup	butter OR margarine	250 mL
½ cup	brown sugar	125 mL
2 tbsp.	white sugar	30 mL
1	egg	1
1 tsp.	vanilla	5 mL
1½ cups	flour	375 mL
½ tsp.	salt	2 mL
1 tsp.	baking soda	5 mL
¼ cup	boiling water	50 mL
2 cups	rolled oats	500 mL
½ cup	chopped nuts (optional)	125 mL
1 cup	semisweet chocolate chips	250 mL

- Beat butter, sugars, egg and vanilla together until light and fluffy.
- In a separate bowl, combine flour and salt. Stir into the creamed mixture.
- Dissolve soda in water. Stir into the creamed mixture.
- Stir in remaining ingredients.
- Drop batter by teaspoonfuls (5 mL) onto ungreased cookie sheets. Flatten with the bottom of a glass dipped in flour.
- Bake at 350°F (180°C) for 12 minutes or until lightly browned.

VARIATIONS   *Smarties or M & M candies may be substituted for the chocolate chips. These will be a hit with the kids.*

YIELD   *4 DOZEN COOKIES*

OATMEAL COCONUT COOKIES

ALTHOUGH A LARGE BATCH, THESE WILL DISAPPEAR VERY QUICKLY!

2 cups	butter OR margarine	500 mL
3 cups	brown sugar	750 mL
2	eggs	2
3 cups	flour	750 mL
2 tsp.	baking powder	10 mL
1 tsp.	baking soda	5 mL
1 tsp.	salt	5 mL
3 cups	rolled oats	750 mL
1½ cups	coconut	375 mL
2 tsp.	vanilla	10 mL
	sugar	

- In a mixing bowl, cream together butter and sugar. Beat in eggs.
- Sift together flour, baking powder, baking soda and salt. Mix into the creamed mixture.
- Add rolled oats, coconut and vanilla. Combine thoroughly.
- Shape dough into balls and place on lightly greased cookie sheets. Press balls down with a fork dipped in sugar.
- Bake at 350°F (180°C) for 10-12 minutes or until lightly browned.

YIELD   *APPROXIMATELY 10 DOZEN COOKIES*

CHERRY COCONUT BARS

PERFECT FOR HOLIDAY ENTERTAINING

BASE:

½ cup	butter	125 mL
1½ cups	flour	375 mL
2 tbsp.	sugar	30 mL
½ tsp.	salt	2 mL

TOPPING:

2	eggs	2
1½ cups	brown sugar	375 mL
2 tbsp.	flour	30 mL
1 tsp.	baking powder	5 mL
½ cup	chopped walnuts	125 mL
½ cup	coconut	125 mL
1 cup	halved glacéed cherries	250 mL

- To prepare base, mix all ingredients together. Press into a greased 9" (23 cm) square pan. Bake at 350°F (180°C) for 10 minutes.
- To prepare filling, beat eggs, then fold in the remaining ingredients. Spread over base. Bake at 325°F (160°C) for 30-35 minutes.
- If desired, frost with Butter Icing, page 158, flavored with lemon juice, omit cocoa.

YIELD   **24 BARS**

COCONUT RASPBERRY BAR

WHIP THIS UP FOR UNEXPECTED COMPANY

1 cup	flour	250 mL
½ cup	butter	125 mL
1 tbsp.	milk	15 mL
1 tsp.	baking powder	5 mL
1	egg	1
½ cup	raspberry jam	125 mL
1 cup	sugar	250 mL
1	egg	1
2 cups	coconut	500 mL
2 tbsp.	melted butter	30 mL
1 tsp.	vanilla	5 mL

- In a mixing bowl, combine flour, butter, milk, baking powder and egg. Spread mixture in a greased 9" (23 cm) square pan.
- Spread raspberry jam over the base.
- In another bowl, beat sugar and egg until frothy. Add coconut, butter and vanilla. Beat well. Spread on top of jam.
- Bake at 350°F (180°C) for 30-40 minutes or until golden brown.

YIELD   24 BARS

MATRIMONIAL SQUARES

AN OLD-FASHIONED TREAT THAT WAS A MUST ON EVERY DESSERT TRAY

DATE FILLING:

2 cups	chopped dates	500 mL
¾ cup	corn syrup	175 mL
½ cup	water	125 mL
½ tsp.	vanilla	2 mL
2 tbsp.	lemon juice	30 mL

BASE AND TOPPING:

1⅓ cups	flour	325 mL
1⅓ cups	brown sugar	325 mL
½ tsp.	baking soda	2 mL
1⅓ cups	rolled oats	325 mL
⅔ cup	melted butter	150 mL

- To prepare date filling, combine all ingredients in a saucepan. Bring to a boil. Simmer until thick and soft, about 15 minutes. Cool.
- To prepare base, mix flour and sugar together. Stir in baking soda and oats. Blend in butter. Mix until crumbly.
- Press half of the base mixture into a greased 9" (23 cm) square pan.
- Spread prepared, cooled date filling over crumbs.
- Cover filling with the remaining half of the crumbs. Pat down until smooth.
- Bake at 350°F (180°C) for 30-35 minutes or until golden brown.

YIELD   24 BARS

VARIATIONS

RAISIN FILLING:

2 cups	seedless raisins	500 mL
2 cups	water	500 mL
½ cup	sugar	125 mL
2 tbsp.	flour	30 mL
⅛ tsp.	salt	0.5 mL
½ tsp.	vanilla	2 mL
1 tbsp.	butter	15 mL
1 tbsp.	lemon juice	15 mL

- Combine raisins and water in a saucepan, simmer for 10 minutes.
- In a mixing bowl, combine sugar, flour and salt. Gradually stir into raisins. Cook and stir over low heat until the mixture is thick.
- Blend in vanilla, butter and lemon juice. Cool.

MATRIMONIAL SQUARES
(CONTINUED)

MINCEMEAT FILLING:

Spread bottom layer of crumbs with 2-2½ cups (500-750 mL) of mincemeat. Top with remaining crumbs. Use Mincemeat recipe on page 175 or 176.

LEMON SQUARES
THESE WILL BECOME A FAMILY FAVORITE

2 cups	flour	500 mL
1 cup	butter	250 mL
½ cup	icing sugar	125 mL
4	eggs	4
2 cups	sugar	500 mL
⅓ cup	lemon juice	75 mL
1 tsp.	lemon rind	5 mL
¼ cup	flour	50 mL
¼ tsp.	baking powder	1 mL
¼ tsp.	salt	1 mL
¼ cup	icing sugar	50 mL

- In a mixing bowl, combine flour, butter and icing sugar. Press into the bottom of a greased 9 x 13" (23 x 33 cm) pan. Bake at 350°F (180°C) for 20 minutes.
- While base is baking, beat eggs and combine with sugar, lemon juice and lemon rind.
- In another bowl, sift together the flour, baking powder and salt. Mix in with the lemon mixture.
- When base is removed from oven, pour over lemon mixture. Return to the oven and continue baking for another 25 minutes.
- Dust with icing sugar while still warm.

YIELD   36 BARS

CHOCOLATE BROWNIES
EVERYBODY'S FAVORITE

½ cup	butter	125 mL
1 cup	brown sugar	250 mL
2	eggs	2
¾ cup	flour	175 mL
3 tbsp.	cocoa	45 mL
½ tsp.	baking powder	2 mL
¼ tsp.	salt	1 mL
½ tsp.	vanilla	2 mL
½ cup	walnuts (optional)	125 mL

- In a mixing bowl, beat together the butter and sugar. Add the eggs and beat well.
- In another bowl, combine the flour, cocoa, baking powder and salt. Stir into the creamed mixture.
- Stir in the vanilla and walnuts.
- Spread into a greased 9" (23 cm) square pan.
- Bake at 375°F (190°C) for 12-15 minutes.
- Cool, then spread with Chocolate Butter Icing, recipe follows.

YIELD   *24 BARS*

CHOCOLATE BUTTER ICING

2 tbsp.	cocoa	30 mL
2 tbsp.	melted butter	30 mL
2 tbsp.	milk	30 mL
1 cup	icing sugar	250 mL

- Combine all ingredients and mix well.
- Makes enough to frost Brownies or a single layer cake.

NANAIMO BARS

A LASTING FAVORITE WITH MANY VARIATIONS!

BASE:

½ cup	butter	125 mL
¼ cup	sugar	50 mL
⅓ cup	cocoa	75 mL
1 tsp.	vanilla	5 mL
1	egg, beaten	1
1 cup	coconut	250 mL
2 cups	graham wafer crumbs	500 mL
½ cup	chopped almonds	125 mL

FILLING

¼ cup	softened butter	50 mL
2 tbsp.	custard powder	30 mL
3 tbsp.	milk	45 mL
2 cups	icing sugar	500 mL
1 tsp.	vanilla	5 mL

GLAZE:

1 tbsp.	butter	15 mL
2 oz.	chocolate (2 squares)	60 g

- To prepare the base, combine butter, sugar, cocoa, vanilla and egg in a saucepan. Heat together, stirring constantly until mixture begins to thicken. Remove from heat.
- Stir coconut, crumbs and almonds into butter mixture in saucepan.
- Spread evenly in a greased 9" (23 cm) square pan.
- To prepare filling, combine all ingredients. Spread on top of base.
- Chill until firm.
- To make glaze, melt butter and chocolate over hot water and spread over filling.

VARIATIONS   *Peanut Butter Nanaimo Bars:*
Base: Substitute chopped peanuts for almonds
Filling: Reduce butter to 2 tbsp. (30 mL) and add ½ cup (125 mL) of peanut butter. Increase milk to 4 tbsp. (60 mL)

Cherry Almond Nanaimo Bars:
Filling: Substitute 2 tbsp. (30 mL) cherry juice for the milk. Substitute 1 tsp. (5 mL) almond extract for the vanilla. Add ⅓ cup (75 mL) of chopped red maraschino cherries.

YIELD   *24 BARS*

PUFFED WHEAT SQUARES

EVERY CHILD'S FAVORITE AND CHILD'S PLAY TO MAKE!

10 cups	puffed wheat	2.5 L
1 cup	brown sugar	250 mL
½ cup	corn syrup	125 mL
¼ cup	butter	50 mL
2 tsp.	cocoa	10 mL
2 tsp.	vanilla	10 mL

- Pour puffed wheat into a large bowl.
- In a saucepan, combine the remaining ingredients. Bring to a boil and continue to boil for 1 minute. Pour over puffed wheat. Mix well.
- Spread into a buttered 9 x 13" (23 x 32 cm) pan. Cool. Cut into squares.

YIELD   *16 SERVINGS*

CHRISTMAS CREATIONS

Revel in the luxury of all of your favorite Christmas treats gathered here. Holiday entertaining and gift-from-your-kitchen ideas make your Christmas season a pleasure. Here are easy, elegant and delicious holiday recipes.

EGGNOG

PLEASE THE FAMILY ON CHRISTMAS EVE WITH THIS ONE!

6	eggs, separated	6
⅛ tsp.	salt	0.5 mL
¼ cup	sugar	50 mL
1 cup	chilled whipping cream	250 mL
¼ cup	sugar	50 mL
1 cup	milk	250 mL
3 cups	ginger ale	750 mL
1 tsp.	nutmeg	5 mL

- Beat egg whites with salt until stiff but not dry. Gradually beat in ¼ cup (50 mL) sugar.
- Beat whipping cream until stiff.
- Beat egg yolks until thick and light. Add remaining sugar and milk, continue to beat until light and fluffy. Stir in ginger ale and blend well. Fold the egg white mixture and the whipped cream into the egg yolk mixture.
- Pour into a punch bowl and sprinkle with grated nutmeg.

VARIATION *Add ½ cup (125 mL) of rum or brandy to the eggnog mixture.*

YIELD *18-20 CUPS (4.5-5 L)*

See photograph on back cover.

TOURTIÈRE

THIS FRENCH CANADIAN MEAT PIE IS AN EXCELLENT DISH
SERVE FOR A CHRISTMAS OR NEW YEAR'S EVE BUFFET!

	pastry for a 2-crust, 9" (23 cm) pie	
1 lb.	ground pork	500 g
½ cup	water	125 mL
1 cup	chopped onion	250 mL
1	garlic clove, minced	1
1 tsp.	thyme	5 mL
½ tsp.	pepper	2 mL
½ tsp.	salt	2 mL
1 tsp.	cloves	5 mL
1 cup	soft bread crumbs OR	250 mL
	cooked mashed potatoes	

- In a saucepan, combine pork, water, onions and garlic. Simmer for 1 hour. Drain off the fat.
- Stir in spices and bread crumbs.
- Line a 9" (23 cm) pie plate with pastry. Fill with pork mixture. Top with pie crust. Seal pastry edges and cut small steam vents in top crust.
- Bake at 375°F (190°C) for 30 minutes or until crust is lightly browned.

YIELD   **8 SERVINGS**

CHRISTMAS PEPPER JELLY
UNUSUALLY HOT AND COOL! A GREAT GIFT IDEA!

2 cups	ground sweet red and green peppers	500 mL
½ cup	ground seeded jalapeño peppers	125 mL
6 cups	sugar	1.5 L
1½ cups	cider vinegar	375 mL
6 oz.	liquid pectin	170 g
	green food coloring (optional)	

- Combine peppers and divide into 2 parts. To ½ of the peppers stir in 1 cup (250 mL) sugar.
- In a saucepan, combine the pepper and sugar mixture with the vinegar and the remaining sugar. Boil for 10 minutes.
- Add the other ½ of peppers and pectin. Boil for an additional 10 minutes.
- Pour into sterilized jars and seal.
- Serve over cream cheese with crackers.

VARIATIONS   *For the Christmas season add green food coloring.*

YIELD   ***8 CUPS (2 L)***

See photograph opposite page 64.

JALAPEÑO CHEESE BALL
WHAT A TREAT FOR A PARTY!

5	jalapeño peppers	5
1 lb.	Cheddar cheese, grated	500 g
½ cup	grated onion	125 mL
1	garlic clove, minced	1
½ cup	mayonnaise	125 mL
1 cup	chopped pecans or parsley	250 mL

- Remove tops and seeds from peppers, and grate finely.
- Combine grated pepper with cheese, onion, garlic and mayonnaise.
- Form into a ball and chill well. Roll in pecans or parsley. Chill again.
- Serve with crackers.

See photograph on back cover.

SPINACH DIP IN BREAD

A GREAT CROWD PLEASER THAT IS EQUALLY DELICIOUS SERVED HOT OR COLD!

10 oz.	pkg. frozen chopped spinach	283 g
8 oz.	cream cheese	250 g
1 cup	grated Cheddar cheese	250 mL
1 tbsp.	finely chopped fresh dillweed	15 mL
1 cup	mayonnaise	250 mL
1 cup	sour cream	250 mL
¼ cup	chopped green onion	50 mL
10 oz.	can water chestnuts, drained and chopped	284 g
1	large loaf of French, Italian round OR pumpernickel bread	1

- Thaw spinach. Drain thoroughly, squeeze dry and chop finely.
- Cream the cheeses together. Stir in the spinach and the remaining ingredients, except the bread.
- Cut a thick slice from the top of the loaf of bread, keeping top intact. Scoop out the remaining part of the loaf, leaving about ½" (1.3 cm) shell. Cut the scooped out part into 1" (2.5 cm) pieces and reserve. Fill the hollow portion of loaf with spinach dip. Replace lid.
- If serving heated, wrap in aluminum foil and bake at 300°F (150°C) for 2 hours.
- To serve, break the lid into 1" (2.5 cm) pieces and place along with the reserved pieces around the loaf. Use these pieces to dip into the spinach mixture.

VARIATIONS   *Substitute cottage cheese for the mayonnaise or sour cream.*
Bacon bits and herbs may be added, if desired.

YIELD   ***FILLING FOR 1 LARGE OR 2 SMALL LOAVES OF BREAD.***

See photograph on back cover.

HINTS   *Prepare spinach filling a day in advance to allow flavors to blend.*

STUFFED MUSHROOMS
A COCKTAIL PARTY PLEASER

8 oz.	cream cheese	250 g
6.5 oz.	can crabmeat	184 g
2	garlic cloves, minced	2
¼ tsp.	salt	1 mL
¼ tsp.	pepper	1 mL
⅛ tsp.	cayenne pepper	0.5 mL
24	medium mushroom caps	24
¼ cup	melted butter	50 mL

• Blend cheese, crabmeat, garlic and spices until soft and thoroughly mixed. Spoon mixture into mushroom caps. Brush melted butter over the caps.
• Bake at 325°F (160°C) for ½ hour or until slightly brown. Serve hot.

YIELD   **24 APPETIZERS**

See photograph on back cover.

SMOKED SALMON PATÉ
INTERESTING SERVED ON CRACKERS, PITA BREAD OR PUMPERNICKLE

½	medium onion	½
8 oz.	cooked salmon	250 g
½ tsp.	liquid smoke	2 mL
8 oz.	cream cheese	250 g
2 tbsp.	lemon juice	30 mL
1 tsp.	finely chopped dillweed	5 mL
	parsley for garnish	
	lemon slices for garnish	

• Finely chop onion in blender. Add remaining ingredients; blend until smooth. Chill.
• Garnish with parsley and lemon slices. Serve with crackers and melba toast.

HINTS   *Mushrooms should be refrigerated in a brown paper bag. This lets them breathe while retaining the humidity to keep them fresh.*

Canned salmon, mixed with ¼ tsp. (1 mL) ground pepper and 1 tsp. (5 mL) of lemon juice, may be substituted for smoked salmon.

CRAB MOUSSE

ALWAYS A HIT AS A PARTY STARTER

1 tbsp.	unflavored gelatin (7 g pkg)	15 mL
¼ cup	cold water	50 mL
½ cup	boiling water	125 mL
½ cup	mayonnaise	125 mL
2 tbsp.	finely chopped fresh dillweed	30 mL
2 tbsp.	finely chopped fresh chives (optional)	30 mL
1 tbsp.	finely chopped onion	15 mL
1 tbsp.	lemon juice	15 mL
3	drops Tabasco sauce	3
½ tsp.	salt	2 mL
¼ tsp.	paprika	1 mL
2 cups	flaked crabmeat	500 mL
1 cup	whipping cream, whipped	250 mL

- In a large mixing bowl, sprinkle the gelatin over the cold water. Let sit for 5 minutes.
- Stir in the boiling water. Mix well until the gelatin dissolves. Cool gelatin to room temperature.
- Add the remaining ingredients except crabmeat and whipping cream. Mix to blend well. Refrigerate until mixture just begins to set.
- Fold in the crabmeat.
- Fold the whipped cream into the mixture.
- Pour into a 6-cup (1.5 L) clear glass bowl or lightly oiled mold.
- Unmold, garnish and serve with an assortment of crackers.

YIELD   *10-12 APPETIZER SERVINGS*

See photograph on back cover.

LAYERED CHRISTMAS SALAD

A COLORFUL SALAD FOR THE CHRISTMAS TABLE!

FIRST LAYER:

| 3 oz. | pkg. lime gelatin | 85 g |
| 14 oz. | pineapple tidbits, drained, reserve juice | 398 mL |

SECOND LAYER:

8 oz.	cream cheese	250 g
¼ cup	Cool Whip	50 mL
¼ cup	mayonnaise	50 mL
1 tbsp.	unflavored gelatin (7 g pkg.)	15 mL
¼ cup	cold water	50 mL
⅔ cup	reserved pineapple juice	150 mL

THIRD LAYER:

| 3 oz. | pkg. strawberry gelatin | 85 g |

- Make lime gelatin according to package directions but use ½ cup (125 mL) less water. Add pineapple. Pour into a clear glass bowl (large enough to accomodate all 3 layers). Cool to set.
- To prepare the second layer, cream together cream cheese, Cool Whip and mayonnaise. In a small bowl, dissolve gelatin in cold water. In a saucepan, bring reserved pineapple juice to a boil. Remove from heat and add to the gelatin mixture. Stir into the cream cheese mixture. Pour on top of set lime layer. Chill to set.
- To prepare third layer, make strawberry gelatin according to package directions but use ½ cup (125 mL) less water. Pour on top of set cheese layer. Chill to set.

HINTS   *In preparing layered jellied salads, pour partially set gelatin onto a spoon back which helps guide and spread liquid over set layer.*

BAKED SWEET POTATO

A MUST FOR CHRISTMAS DINNER!

3 cups	cooked, mashed sweet potato	750 mL
½ cup	brown sugar	125 mL
2	eggs	2
¼ cup	milk	50 mL
¼ cup	melted butter	50 mL

TOPPING:

½ cup	brown sugar	125 mL
⅓ cup	flour	75 mL
¼ cup	melted butter	50 mL
1 cup	chopped pecans	250 mL

- Combine sweet potato, sugar, eggs, milk and butter. Place in a buttered 2-quart (2 L) ovenproof casserole.
- Combine the topping ingredients. Mix well. Sprinkle on top of potato mixture.
- Bake, covered, at 350°F (180°C) for 1 hour or until thoroughly heated.

This dish may be prepared early in the day and heated just prior to serving.

YIELD   6-8 SERVINGS

See photograph opposite page 96.

GLAZED HAM

5 lb.	smoked ham	2.2 kg
1 tbsp.	whole cloves	15 mL
14 oz.	can sliced pineapple	398 mL
⅓ cup	halved red and green glacéed cherries	75 mL
⅓ cup	brown sugar	75 mL
½ tsp.	Dijon mustard	2 mL

- Place ham on a rack in roasting pan. Score ham fat in a crisscross pattern. Press cloves into ham where lines intersect.
- Drain pineapple, reserving the juice. Arrange pineapple slices with cherry halves on ham. If necessary, secure with toothpicks.
- Combine sugar, mustard and 2 tbsp. (30 mL) of reserved juice. Slowly drizzle over ham.
- Bake at 325°F (160°C) for 2 hours. Occasionally baste with juice.

YIELD   8 SERVINGS

ROAST TURKEY

BASIC PREPARATION:

1. In purchasing a turkey allow ½-¾ lb. (250-365 g) eviscerated whole turkey per serving.
2. If frozen, thaw turkey according to directions on turkey bag. Like fresh turkeys, thawed turkeys should be refrigerated and used within 2 days.
3. To prepare for roasting, rinse turkey under cold running water. Examine body cavity and discard parts of inner organs that were not thoroughly removed. Dry thoroughly inside and out.
4. Simmer the giblets and neck in lightly salted water for 2 hours or until tender. Use in soup, gravy or dressing.
5. Place turkey, breast side up, on a rack in a roasting pan. If the bird is large a lifting cradle is a convenient device on which to place the bird to allow for easier removal when roasting is complete.
6. Season turkey cavity or stuff turkey with a selected dressing, see page 171. Allow ½-¾ cup (125-175 mL) of stuffing per pound (500 g) of turkey. If preferred, stuffing may be baked in a casserole separate from the bird for approximately 1 hour. In this case, additional water or turkey broth is added. If extra stuffing is prepared, stuff the turkey and cook the remainder separately. Stuff the turkey just prior to roasting. Never stuff the bird in advance of roasting. Stuff the neck and body cavities loosely to allow for expansion during roasting. Draw the neck skin over the stuffed neck cavity and fasten to the back with skewers. Close opening of the body cavity by placing 2 end slices of bread over dressing. Return legs and tail to the original tucked position.
7. Cover with roaster cover or with aluminum foil, left loose at the sides but tucked under bird at ends. During last hour of roasting, uncover and baste several times. Roast according to following roasting timetable. Many factors affect the roasting times of turkeys so use the timetable only as an approximate.
8. To test for doneness, the legs should move readily when twisted. Also, the thick part of the drumstick will feel soft if the turkey is done.
9. Remove turkey from oven. Cover. Let bird "rest" for 20 minutes before carving and serving.

ROAST TURKEY
(CONTINUED)

ROASTING TIMETABLE FOR TURKEY

For oven set at 325°F (160°C)

Eviscerated ready-to-cook weight: in lbs.	in kg: (averaged)	* Stuffed bird (approximate time) in hours:
6 - 8	3	4 Hours
10 - 12	5	5 hours
14 - 16	7	6 hours
18 - 20	9	7 hours
22 - 24	10	9 hours

* If turkey is not stuffed, deduct approximately 5 minutes per pound (10 minutes per kilogram) from the above times.

TURKEY DRESSING

½ cup	butter	125 mL
¾ cup	chopped onion	175 mL
1½ cups	chopped celery	375 mL
½ lb.	pork sausage meat	250 g
10 cups	coarse bread crumbs	2.5 L
1 tbsp.	salt	15 mL
1 tsp.	pepper	5 mL
1 tbsp.	sage OR thyme OR marjoram	15 mL
2 tsp.	poultry seasoning	10 mL
	hot water	

- In a deep skillet, melt butter and sauté onion and celery. Stir in sausage meat and continue to cook until meat is broken up and well mixed with the vegetables.
- In a large mixing bowl, combine bread crumbs with seasonings. Stir in vegetable-meat mixture. Add hot water to mixture, until the dressing clings together.

YIELD   *MAKES ENOUGH DRESSING TO STUFF THE CAVITY OF A 12-15 LB. (5-7 KG) TURKEY.*

CRANBERRY SAUCE

A GREAT CLASSIC PLUS AN INTERESTING VARIATION

2 cups	fresh OR frozen cranberries	500 mL
1 cup	boiling water	250 mL
1 cup	sugar	250 mL

- In a saucepan, cover cranberries with water. Bring to a boil, cover, and continue to boil gently for a few minutes or until the cranberry skins burst.
- Add sugar. Return to a full rolling boil. Remove from heat and set to cool.

VARIATIONS   *Cut rind from orange. Chop rind finely. Discard pits and membrances. Chop fruit pulp finely. Add rind and pulp to cranberries and water.*

YIELD   *A GENEROUS 2 CUPS (500 ML)*

TURKEY STOCK

1	turkey carcass	1
	water	
1	large onion, chopped	1
1 cup	chopped celery	250 mL
1 cup	diced carrots	250 mL
½ cup	chopped cabbage (optional)	125 mL
1 tsp.	salt	5 mL
½ tsp.	pepper	2 mL

- Place turkey carcass in large soup kettle. Cover with water. Add remaining ingredients. Bring to a boil, cover, reduce heat, simmer for 2-3 hours. Strain. Reserve stock. Cool strained ingredients slightly and separate turkey meat from remainder. Dice turkey meat and use in soup.

HINTS   *Cook cranberries just until their skins burst. Further cooking makes them bitter tasting.*

If turkey stock is thoroughly chilled, any fat will harden as a layer on the top. Remove this before using stock in soup or other recipes.

Refrigerate stock and use within 2 days or freeze in small portions for use in various recipes.

TURKEY SOUP

GRANDMA'S BOXING DAY SPECIAL FOR HER GUESTS!

6 cups	turkey stock	1.5 L
2 cups	cooked diced turkey	500 mL
1	onion, chopped	1
1	garlic clove, minced	1
¼ cup	chopped celery	50 mL
2	medium carrots, diced	2
½ tsp.	salt	2 mL
½ tsp.	pepper	2 mL
2 tbsp.	chopped parsley	30 mL
1	bay leaf	1
1	potato, peeled and diced	1
1 cup	whipping cream	250 mL

- Place all ingredients, except cream, in a large soup kettle. Simmer for 2-3 hours or until vegetables are tender. Remove bay leaf.
- Stir in cream. Heat thoroughly. Serve hot.

VARIATIONS   *Various vegetables may be added in bite-sized pieces.*
Rice, pearl barley or small-sized pasta may be added if desired.
Add additional stock to obtain desired consistency.

YIELD   **6 SERVINGS**

TURKEY À LA KING

EITHER CHICKEN OR TURKEY MAKES THIS A ROYAL DISH!

⅓ cup	butter	75 mL
¼ lb.	mushrooms, sliced	125 g
¼ cup	chopped onion	50 mL
¼ cup	chopped celery	50 mL
¼ cup	chopped green pepper	50 mL
¼ cup	flour	50 mL
1 tsp.	salt	5 mL
1 cup	chicken broth	250 mL
1 cup	milk	250 mL
2 cups	diced cooked turkey (or chicken)	500 mL
2 tbsp.	chopped pimiento	30 mL

- In a skillet, melt butter; add mushrooms, onion, celery and green pepper; cook until vegetables are tender. Remove vegetables with a slotted spoon. Set aside.
- To butter in skillet, blend in flour and salt. Heat until mixture bubbles. Remove from heat.
- While stirring constantly, gradually add chicken broth and milk. Return to heat. Bring to a boil. Cook an additional 2 minutes. Reduce heat.
- To sauce, add reserved vegetables, turkey and pimiento. Cook until thoroughly heated.
- Serve hot on split baking powder biscuits, page 13, toast or rice.

YIELD   *6 SERVINGS*

ENGLISH MINCEMEAT

A CHRISTMAS TRADITION — THE EARLIEST VERSIONS WERE MADE WITH MINCED VENISON OR BEEF.

1	lemon	1
1	orange	1
1 lb.	seedless raisins	500 g
½ lb.	sultana raisins	250 g
1 lb.	currants	500 g
¼ lb.	chopped mixed peel	125 g
2 lbs.	apples, chopped	1 kg
1 lb.	sugar	500 g
1 tsp.	cinnamon	5 mL
½ tsp.	nutmeg	2 mL
½ tsp.	mace	2 mL
½ tsp.	salt	2 mL
1 lb.	suet, finely chopped	500 g

- Grate the lemon and orange rinds. Squeeze out the juices.
- Wash and dry raisins and currants.
- In a large mixing bowl, combine the rind, juice, raisins, currants, peel, apples, sugar and spices.
- Stir in the suet.
- Pack into sterile jars. Seal. Store in a cool place or put in large container and keep refrigerated until ready to use. This mincemeat should be made at least 6-8 weeks before Christmas.

YIELD   *14 CUPS (3.5 L)*

See photograph on back cover, in Mincemeat Tarts.

GREEN TOMATO MINCEMEAT

NO SUET BUT EQUALLY DELICIOUS!

12 cups	coarsely chopped green tomatoes	3 L
1 tbsp.	pickling salt	15 mL
4 cups	brown sugar	1 L
3 cups	seedless raisins	750 mL
2 cups	halved candied cherries	500 mL
1 cup	currants	250 mL
1 cup	chopped mixed candied peel	250 mL
1 cup	cider, white wine, apple juice OR brandy	250 mL
½ cup	cider vinegar	125 mL
½ cup	butter	125 mL
¼ cup	lemon juice	50 mL
2 tsp.	finely grated lemon rind	10 mL
1 tsp.	cloves	5 mL
1 tsp.	mace	5 mL
1 tsp.	cinnamon	5 mL
1 tsp.	nutmeg	5 mL
1 tsp.	allspice	5 mL

- Place tomatoes in a large kettle. Sprinkle with pickling salt and let stand for 1 hour.
- Drain tomatoes. Rinse with cold water. Drain again. Return to kettle.
- Add remaining ingredients to kettle. Bring mixture to a boil, stirring frequently. Reduce heat and simmer for about 2 hours or until mixture is thick and dark brown. Stir often while simmering. Cool.
- Refrigerate for up to 2 months or freeze or pack in sterile jars and seal for longer storage.
- Use for mincemeat pies, tarts, matrimonial squares, page 156, or other favorite recipes.

YIELD   *4 QUARTS (4 L)*

CARROT PUDDING

A LOT OF LOVE GOES INTO MAKING THIS TRADITIONAL CHRISTMAS RECIPE
AND YOUR FAMILY WILL LOVE YOU FOR IT!

1 cup	grated carrots	250 mL
1 cup	grated apples	250 mL
1 cup	grated potatoes	250 mL
½ cup	melted butter	125 mL
1 cup	brown sugar	250 mL
2 cups	raisins	500 mL
1 cup	flour	250 mL
1 tsp.	nutmeg	5 mL
1 tsp.	cinnamon	5 mL
1 tsp.	salt	5 mL
1 tsp.	soda	5 mL
1 tbsp.	lemon juice	15 mL

- In a large pan, combine the above ingredients until thoroughly mixed.
- Spoon into 1-quart (1 L) jars filling only ¾ full. Seal. Place in a water bath in canner. Boil for 3 hours.
- To serve, reheat and serve with Rum Sauce, recipe follows.

VARIATIONS *Mixed fruit may be added if desired. Also, suet may replace the butter.*

YIELD *3 QUARTS (3 L)*

RUM SAUCE:

½ cup	butter	125 mL
¾ cup	brown sugar	175 mL
¼ cup	cream	50 mL
½ tsp.	rum-flavored extract OR 2 tbsp. (30 mL) rum	2 mL

- In a saucepan, melt butter. Add the brown sugar. Mix well. Boil for 2 minutes.
- Add cream and boil 2 minutes longer. Remove from heat.
- Add rum flavoring. Mix well. Serve on carrot or other puddings.

LIGHT FRUIT CAKE

RICH, MOIST, AND FULL OF FRUIT

8 oz.	diced candied pineapple	250 g
1 lb.	red glacéed cherries	500 g
1 lb.	green glacéed cherries	500 g
2 lbs.	light raisins	1 kg
1 lb.	mixed cut peel	500 g
1 lb.	whole blanched almonds	500 g
½ cup	brandy	125 mL
1 lb.	butter at room temperature	500 g
1 cup	sugar	250 mL
8	eggs	8
5 cups	flour	1.25 L
1 cup	apple juice	250 mL
1 tsp.	almond extract	5 mL

- In a very large bowl, soak the fruit and almonds in brandy overnight.
- The next morning, in a large mixing bowl, cream together the butter and sugar until light. Add the eggs and beat until well blended. Add the flour, juice and almond extract; beat until batter is smooth.
- Stir egg batter into soaked fruits. Mix well.
- Prepare 3, 5 x 9" (13 x 23 cm) loaf pans by lining them with buttered heavy-duty waxed paper or brown paper. Turn batter into pans.
- Bake on centre rack at 300°F (150°C) for 30 minutes. Reduce oven heat to 250°F (120°C) and continue baking for an additional 3 hours. During baking time have a pan of hot water in the bottom of the oven. Replenish this water if it evaporates during baking.

NOTE   *This recipe contains no baking powder.*

YIELD   *3 LOAVES*

See photograph on back cover.

WARTIME CHRISTMAS CAKE
MANY A SOLDIER WAITED FOR THIS TREAT DURING THE WAR

1 lb.	raisins	500 g
1½ cups	water	375 mL
1½ cups	sugar	375 mL
1 cup	butter	250 mL
6	eggs	6
2½ cups	flour	625 mL
2½ tsp.	baking powder	12 mL
¼ tsp.	salt	1 mL
½ tsp.	baking soda	2 mL
½ tsp.	cloves	2 mL
1 tsp.	cinnamon	5 mL
1 cup	chopped nuts	250 mL
1 cup	halved glacéed cherries	250 mL

- In a saucepan, combine raisins, water and sugar. Bring to a boil, reduce heat and cook for 5 minutes. Remove from heat. Add butter. Stir to blend. Set aside to cool.
- In a large mixing bowl, beat eggs until fluffy. Add cooled raisin mixture.
- Combine flour, baking powder, salt, baking soda, cloves and cinnamon. Stir in nuts and cherries. Add to raisin mixture. Stir to mix well.
- Prepare 3, 5 x 9" (13 x 23 cm) loaf pans by lining them with buttered heavy-duty waxed paper or brown paper. Turn batter into pans.
- Bake on center rack at 300°F (150°C) for 30 minutes. Reduce oven heat to 250°F (120°C) and continue baking for an additional 2½ hours. During baking time, have a pan of hot water in the bottom of the oven. Replenish this water if it evaporates during baking.

YIELD   3 LOAVES

CHERRY-ALMOND BUNDT CAKE

A LIGHT ALTERNATIVE TO THE TRADITIONAL CHRISTMAS CAKE

2 cups	halved red and green candied cherries	500 mL
½ cup	slivered almonds	125 mL
½ cup	flour	125 mL
1 cup	butter OR margarine	250 mL
½ cup	sugar	125 mL
1 tsp.	vanilla extract	5 mL
1 tsp.	almond extract	5 mL
4	eggs	4
1½ cups	flour	375 mL
2 tsp.	baking powder	10 mL
½ tsp.	salt	2 mL
⅓ cup	milk	75 mL

- Combine cherries and almonds with ½ cup (125 mL) flour, until fruit is well coated.
- Cream butter, sugar and flavorings, until light and fluffy.
- Add eggs, 1 at a time, to butter mixture beating well after each addition.
- Combine dry ingredients. Add alternately with milk to creamed mixture.
- Stir in fruit and nuts.
- Turn into a greased and floured 10-cup (2.5 L) bundt pan. Bake at 350°F (180°C) for 55 minutes or until cake tests done.
- Cool in pan for 10 minutes. Turn out on wire rack to cool.
- Store in a cool place for several days to allow cake to ripen.

VARIATIONS   *Substitute alternate fruits and/or nuts, try candied mixed fruit or dried apricots and walnuts or pecans, or use your own favorites.*

YIELD   *16 SERVINGS*

EGGNOG BARS

AN EXCELLENT WAY TO USE LEFTOVER EGGNOG

½ cup	butter OR margarine	125 mL
1 cup	sugar	250 mL
1 tsp.	rum flavoring	5 mL
2¼ cups	flour	550 mL
1 tsp.	baking soda	5 mL
¼ tsp.	nutmeg	1 mL
¼ tsp.	salt	1 mL
1 cup	eggnog	250 mL
1 cup	chopped maraschino cherries	250 mL
½ cup	chopped toasted almonds	125 mL

- Cream butter and sugar until fluffy. Blend in flavoring.
- Combine flour, soda, nutmeg and salt.
- Add dry ingredients, alternately with eggnog, to creamed mixture.
- Stir in cherries and nuts.
- Spread batter in a greased 10 x 15" (25 x 40 cm) jelly-roll pan.
- Bake at 350°F (180°C) for 18-20 minutes or until golden brown.
- Drizzle icing over warm cake. Cool. Cut into bars.

ICING:

¾ cup	icing sugar	175 mL
½ tsp.	rum flavoring	2 mL
3-4 tsp.	milk	15-20 mL
	few drops green food coloring	

- Mix all ingredients until smooth.
- Drizzle over warm cake.

YIELD   *48 BARS*

PECAN BUTTER TART SQUARES

BY PREPARING THIS IN 2 PANS, 1 MAY BE ENJOYED NOW
AND THE OTHER MAY BE FROZEN AND ENJOYED LATER

2 cups	flour	500 mL
1 cup	sugar	250 mL
1 cup	butter	250 mL
1½ cups	raisins	375 mL
1 cup	currants	250 mL
2 cups	boiling water	500 mL
4	eggs, lightly beaten	4
2 cups	brown sugar	500 mL
¼ cup	flour	50 mL
1 tsp.	baking powder	5 mL
1 tsp.	vanilla	5 mL
⅛ tsp.	salt	0.5 mL
1 cup	chopped pecans	250 mL

- Combine flour and sugar. Cut in butter until the mixture resembles coarse meal. Spread in 2, 9" (23 cm) square cake pans. Press lightly. Bake at 350°F (180°C) for 15 minutes.
- Combine the raisins and currants. Cover with boiling water and let stand for 10 minutes. Drain and dry fruit.
- Beat together the eggs, sugar, flour, baking powder, vanilla and salt.
- Sprinkle raisins and currants over baked bases. Pour the egg/sugar mixture over.
- Sprinkle chopped pecans over mixture in pans.
- Bake at 350°F (180°C) for 20-25 minutes.

YIELD   *24 BARS PER PAN*

BUTTER TARTS

A FAMILY TRADITION FOR MANY GENERATIONS

	pastry for 24 tarts	
2	eggs	2
2 cups	brown sugar	500 mL
1 tbsp.	vinegar	15 mL
½ cup	melted butter	125 mL
1 tsp.	vanilla	5 mL
1½ cups	currants, raisins, and chopped walnuts in combination	375 mL

- Prepare pastry.
- In a mixing bowl, beat the eggs. Add the sugar, vinegar, butter and vanilla. Beat together until foamy.
- Add fruit and/or nuts.
- Pour into unbaked tart shells until ⅔ full.
- Bake at 375°F (190°C) for 20 minutes or until lightly browned.

YIELD   ***2 DOZEN***

See photograph on back cover.

MAPLE SUGAR PIE

ANOTHER FRENCH CANADIAN TRADITION
VERY SWEET, VERY RICH!

	pastry for 1-crust pie, page 133	
1½ cups	maple sugar	375 mL
3	eggs, beaten	3
1 tbsp.	flour	15 mL
¼ tsp.	salt	1 mL
1 cup	whipping OR cereal cream	250 mL
1 tsp.	vanilla OR 1 tbsp. (15 mL) rum (optional)	5 mL
⅓ cup	melted butter	75 mL
	whipped cream (optional)	

- Line a 9" (23 cm) pie plate with pastry.
- Sprinkle maple sugar over pastry.
- Combine beaten eggs, flour, salt, cream and flavoring. Pour gently over sugar and top with melted butter.
- Bake at 450°F (230°C) for 10 minutes. Reduce heat to 300°F (150°C) and bake until filling is just about firm, about 25 minutes.
- Cool before serving. Serve in very small pieces, with whipped cream, if you wish.

YIELD   ***8-10 SERVINGS***

PECAN CRESCENTS
A "MELT-IN-YOUR-MOUTH" DELICACY!

1 cup	butter, room temperature	250 mL
⅓ cup	icing sugar	75 mL
1 tsp.	vanilla	5 mL
2 cups	flour	500 mL
1 cup	finely chopped pecans	250 mL

- In a mixing bowl, cream butter. Add icing sugar and vanilla. Beat well.
- Add flour and chopped pecans. Mix until well blended. Chill dough.
- Form dough into 1" (2.5 cm) balls. Shape into crescent shapes. Place on an ungreased cookie sheet.
- Bake at 325°F (160°C) for 12 minutes or until lightly browned.
- While still warm, roll in icing sugar.

YIELD   *APPROXIMATELY 6 DOZEN*

See photograph on back cover.

CREAM WAFERS
BUTTERY DAINTIES!

1 cup	butter, softened	250 mL
⅓ cup	whipping cream	75 mL
2 cups	flour	500 mL

- Combine ingredients. Mix well, cover and chill.
- Divide dough into thirds. Using ⅓ at a time, roll out on a floured surface to ⅛" (3 mm) thickness. Cut into 1½ " (4 cm) diameter rounds. Place on a cookie sheet. Prick each round with a fork about 4 times.
- Bake at 350°F (180°C) for 7-9 minutes or until just beginning to brown. Cool.
- Put 2 wafers together with Creamy Icing, recipe follows:

CREAMY ICING:

¼ cup	butter OR margarine	50 mL
¾ cup	icing sugar	175 mL
1 tsp.	vanilla	5 mL
5-6	drops of desired food coloring	5-6

- Beat ingredients together until creamy. Put between wafers.

YIELD   *3 DOZEN*

THIMBLE COOKIES

IT WOULDN'T BE CHRISTMAS WITHOUT THESE DELICIOUS MORSELS!

½ cup	butter	125 mL
¼ cup	brown sugar	50 mL
1	egg yolk	1
1 cup	flour	250 mL
1	egg white, beaten	1
1 cup	finely chopped walnuts	250 mL

- In a mixing bowl, combine butter, sugar, egg yolk and flour. Beat well.
- Shape dough into 1" (2.5 cm) balls. Dip in egg white and roll in nuts. Make an indentation in the center of ball with your thumb or a thimble.
- Place on a cookie sheet. Bake at 350°F (180°C) for 10-12 minutes or until lightly browned. Cool.
- Fill indentation with your favorite jam or with half a maraschino cherry.

VARIATIONS   *Substitute any other chopped nut, coconut, crushed cornflakes or Rice Crispies for the walnuts.*

YIELD   *3 DOZEN*
See photograph on back cover.

SHORTBREAD

SIMPLE — PREPARE AHEAD AND FREEZE

1 cup	butter, softened but not oily	250 mL
½ cup	icing sugar	125 mL
2 cups	flour	500 mL

- Cream butter. Add icing sugar. Mix well.
- Add flour gradually, until dough begins to crack.
- Turn dough onto a lightly floured surface. Roll ⅛" (3 mm) thick. Cut out cookies with lightly floured cookie cutters. Transfer cookies to cookie sheets.
- Bake at 300°F (150°C) for 10 minutes or until cookies just begin to brown. Carefully remove cookies to cooling racks.

VARIATIONS   *Decorate with the following or use your favorites, red and green glacéed cherry pieces, almonds, cookie trims, miniature chocolate chips.*

YIELD   *4 DOZEN*
See photograph on back cover.

HINTS   *Use a cookie press to obtain interesting shapes for shortbread.*

Roski

To slovakians, the festive season without these is unimaginable!

1 tbsp.	yeast	15 mL
½ cup	lukewarm water	125 mL
1 tsp.	sugar	5 mL
1	egg	1
11	egg yolks	11
1½ cups	evaporated milk	375 mL
7 cups	flour	1.75 mL
1 tsp.	salt	5 mL
1 lb.	butter, at room temperature	500 g
1½ lbs.	walnuts, finely chopped	750 g
1 cup	sugar	250 mL
1 tbsp.	milk	15 mL
	berry sugar	

- Combine yeast, water and sugar. Let rise for 10 minutes. Add egg, egg yolks and milk. Mix well.
- In a large mixing bowl, combine flour and salt. Add butter. Mix until crumbly. Make a well in crumb mixture. Add egg mixture. Mix and knead until smooth. Let rise a minimum of 4 hours or overnight.
- Divide dough into smaller portions. On a lightly sugared surface, roll out dough until very thin. Cut into 2" (5 cm) squares.
- Combine walnuts, sugar and milk. Place a teaspoonful (5 mL) of walnut mixture near 1 edge of each square. Roll up squares, beginning with filled edge. Roll in berry sugar. Shape into crescent shapes. Place on lightly greased cookie sheet and bake at 350°F (180°C) for 20 minutes or until lightly brown.
- These freeze well so can be made ahead.

YIELD　　　*APPROXIMATELY — 8 DOZEN CRESCENTS*

See photograph on back cover.

HOLIDAY WREATH COOKIES
CHILDREN LOVE TO HELP WITH THESE FESTIVE COOKIES

30	marshmallows	30
½ cup	butter OR margarine	125 mL
1 tsp.	vanilla	5 mL
2 tsp.	green food coloring	10 mL
3½ cups	cornflakes	875 mL
½ cup	small red cinnamon candies	125 mL

- Line 2 large cookie sheets with waxed paper.
- In the top of a double boiler, combine the marshmallows, butter, vanilla and food coloring. Heat over boiling water. Stir frequently, until marshmallows are melted.
- Remove from heat and gradually stir in the cornflakes.
- Drop rounded, greased spoonfuls of marshmallow mixture onto cookie sheets. Shape into 2" (5 cm) wreaths. Decorate with red candies.
- Store between layers of waxed paper in refrigerator.

YIELD   *ABOUT 2½ DOZEN*

CHOCOLATE FUDGE
CHRISTMAS WOULDN'T BE CHRISTMAS WITHOUT THIS!

2 cups	sugar	500 mL
½ cup	butter	125 mL
1 cup	evaporated milk	250 mL
1 cup	semisweet chocolate chips	250 mL
¾ cup	flour	175 mL
1 cup	finely crushed graham cracker crumbs	250 mL
¾ cup	chopped walnuts	175 mL
1 tsp.	vanilla	5 mL

- In a heavy saucepan, combine sugar, butter and milk. Bring to a full boil, stirring constantly. Continue to boil for 10 minutes, stirring occasionally.
- Remove from heat. Stir in the remaining ingredients.
- Spread in a buttered 9" (23 cm) square pan.
- Cool and enjoy.

YIELD   *APPROXIMATELY 60 PIECES*

INDEX

INDEX

INDEX

Share GRANDMA'S TOUCH with a friend

Please send _____ copies of *GRANDMA'S TOUCH* at $19.95 per book, plus $4.00 (total order) for postage and handling.

GRANDMA'S TOUCH _____ x $19.95 = $ _____

Postage and handling _____ = $ 4.00

Subtotal _____ = $ _____

In Canada add 7% GST OR 15% HST where applicable = $ _____

Total enclosed_____ = $ _____

U.S. or International orders payable in U.S. funds.

NAME: _____

STREET: _____

CITY: _____ PROV./STATE: _____

COUNTRY: _____ POSTAL CODE/ZIP: _____

A GREAT GIFT IDEA

Please make cheque or money order payable to:

Centax Books & Distribution
1150 Eighth Avenue
Regina, Saskatchewan
Canada S4R 1C9

For VISA or MASTERCARD orders, mail
                    or toll-free Phone: 1-800-667-5595
                              FAX: 1-800-823-6829
        E-mail: centax@printwest.com www.centaxbooks.com

For fund-raising or volume purchases, contact **Centax Books & Distribution** for volume rates. Please allow 2-3 weeks for delivery.
Price is subject to change.